TAROT

connect with yourself • develop your intuition • live mindfully

TAROT

connect with yourself • develop your intuition • live mindfully

TINA GONG

Senior Editor Emma Hill
Senior Art Editors Collette Sadler,
Karen Constanti
Designer Tessa Bindloss
Editorial Assistant Kiron Gill
Senior Jacket Creative Nicola Powling
Jacket Coordinator Lucy Philpott
Managing Editor Dawn Henderson
Managing Art Editor Marianne Markham
Senior Producer (Pre-Production) Tony Phipps
Senior Producer Luca Bazzoli
Creative Technical Support Sonia Charbonnier
Art Director Maxine Pedliham
Publishing Director Mary-Clare Jerram

Illustrated by Tina Gong

First published in Great Britain in 2020 by
Dorling Kindersley Limited
DK, One Embassy Gardens, 8 Viaduct Gardens,
London, SW11 7BW

The authorised representative in the EEA is
Dorling Kindersley Verlag GmbH. Arnulfstr. 124,
80636 Munich, Germany

A CIP catalogue record for this book
is available from the British Library.
ISBN: 978-0-2414-3323-2

Printed and bound in Slovakia

For the curious
www.dk.com

CONTENTS

FOREWORD

When I was a child, I used to spend my days playing with fierce dragons, exploring the vast reaches of the solar system, and performing songs for a kingdom of various toy animals. All of us have participated in variations of this when we were younger; but as we grow up, we learn to leave this fantastical world of imagination behind.

The older I get, the more I believe those childhood daydreams hold the key for us to live more meaningful lives as adults. When we were young, the boundary between our inner and outer world wasn't so opaque; these worlds existed in unison with one another. Our lives were rich and full of wonder. When we learn to differentiate and separate our inner world from the outer, we lose our innocence. The more palpable the walls become between our inner lives and outer experiences, the more vacant our lives seem, and the harder it is to peer beyond that boundary. This makes us feel empty, fragmented, and isolated, like a part of ourselves is missing.

But that vivid life we once led never really disappears; it lives on, hidden in our unconscious, appearing in dreams and nightmares, and sometimes projected onto other people without us even knowing. And when we react to those projections so intensely, we never know that we are reacting to something that is a part of our self. Reclaiming these projections as part of our own psyche also reclaims our personal

power. It gives us the knowledge of what truly exists, versus what our fears or anxieties have placed there.

Once we re-discover the language of symbols and archetypes – the same language expressed in our dreams, our imagination and, yes, tarot – we unlock a whole new layer of the world; one that is alive and surging with vitality, deeply connected and interwoven, and has the potential to unite us with our environment.

When we tell stories through tarot, we are joining our inner world with our everyday experiences. Through that lens, we find new ways of relating to things that we may otherwise consider mundane, random, or incomprehensible. Hugging a stuffed toy is a

way to comfort your inner child. A stressful routine can be an arduous quest to reach your potential. A confrontation with a difficult person can really be about us recognizing what we dislike and fear the most in ourselves. It is through our ability to tell stories about our experiences, and our own unique journey, that we both discover and create meaning.

Even if it does nothing else for you, it is my hope that working with the tarot is just one path that helps you develop your own symbolic capacity, and find an anchor in an otherwise chaotic and senseless sea.

With love

TAROT THROUGH THE AGES

Tarot has had a long history, evolving from a card game with many variations that were played throughout Europe, to a complex system of esoteric symbols for telling the future, and finally to a mirror of the human psyche.

TAROT AS A GAME

The earliest recorded history of the tarot is from the 1300s, but it was a version with no Major Arcana, only the four suits that would later become the Minor Arcana. "Triumph cards" were added in 1440, and later became known as the Major Arcana. We see the first mention of *tarocchi*, the Italian word for tarot, in the 1500s, when presumably it still took the form of a card game, in which the goal was to earn as many points as possible.

DIVINATORY TAROT

In the late 1700s, occultists began using tarot for divination, so the cards then came to be regarded as fortune-telling devices. The first known tarot reader was Etteilla, a French occultist who popularized tarot divination and created the first tarot deck specifically intended for cartomancy. He also published work detailing the meanings of each card, reversed and upright, and how they correspond to the elements and astrology.

TAROT AND OCCULTISM

French occultist, Eliphas Levi, developed the idea of tarot as a fortune-telling tool in 1856, incorporating the tarot into a holistic esoteric system. This would become the foundation for the Hermetic Order of the Golden Dawn, a school of Western philosophy and magic.

The spread of occultism was largely a reaction to materialism; the idea that all things are dependent on physical processes. As our understanding of the world became increasingly bound to the measurable, occultists felt this world's sterility — and sought instead to integrate science and spirituality. Pure logic, without spirit, does not lead us to happiness or fulfilment. Both are necessary for true purpose and meaning.

Many occultists also sought to distance themselves from Christianity, searching for inspiration in pagan gods, Eastern religions, or both. Their focus was on the spiritual development of the individual, versus the moralistic focus of Christianity. Many esoteric

concepts, like the Tree of Life, tarot, and alchemy are actually metaphorical representations of spiritual development; they are handbooks, if you know how to read them.

TAROT AND THE PSYCHE

Carl Jung was one of the founders of modern psychology, and the creator of the theory of archetypes and the collective unconscious. Modern interpretations of the tarot, such as the ones in this book, can find their origins in his work. Jung believed that the primary goal of every person was something called individuation; the becoming of who one really is, through the conscious integration of all aspects of the self.

If we view tarot through a Jungian lens, each of the cards embodies an archetype. Archetypes come from our collective unconscious, a universal symbolic language within every person. They are primal human blueprints, the lens through which we meet the world. In our everyday lives we see representations of them in gods of every religion, and fairy tales of all cultures. They are characters in stories we read and movies we watch. We find them in the narratives we tell ourselves. And in tarot, they are the many faces of the self that we carry within us, who we must learn to meet without fear, shame, or hate. It is through archetypes that we create images, tell stories, and ultimately derive meaning for our lives.

TAROT AND MINDFULNESS

Your approach to reading the tarot can profoundly change the psychological effect that readings have on you and others. The goal is to use the tarot constructively; as a tool to build inner strength, self-knowledge, and acceptance.

TAROT AS A PSYCHOLOGICAL TOOL

The power of tarot cards is not inherent; they are after all just a series of images printed on paper. Their power comes from us, as readers, and how we relate to these images – it is derived from how we interpret, narrate, and develop the stories we tell with them. The magic is within you; the cards are just a way for you to connect to it.

These cards are best used as a tool for affirming our sense of autonomy, independence, and hope. Even when receiving negative cards in a reading, it is about the flexibility of our minds and our hearts enabling us to re-direct our actions and choices towards something positive. Learning to read the cards in a mindful manner is a lesson in channelling emotions. The events in our lives are like tarot cards; they can be random and chaotic. Life is unfair sometimes; we can have a lucky draw or an awful hand, but where we choose to direct our energy, emotions, and resources can transform events into something that either pushes us towards our peak, or triggers our worst impulses. How we choose to react to what life deals us is everything.

RITUALS

Ritual and ceremony are integral parts of human behaviour. They are, like the tarot, symbolic, where we connect the physical world with our inner space. For example, when we cleanse our home with sage, it is a symbolic act of cleansing our spirit.

Rituals affect us on a raw, instinctual level. When we use our hands and all our senses with symbolic intention in mind, we are erasing the boundary between what is within us and without. It is a way of effecting change and reclaiming power when we feel powerless, and connecting with the symbolic world of archetypes that are hidden within us – like we do when we recite a mantra or a prayer, for example. When you see the cards, and you hold them in your hands, imagine holding the events of your life within those cards. This symbolic understanding of the tarot is key to experiencing its power.

COMMUNICATING WITH THE TAROT

As you sit with the cards, don't think only in terms of them sending a message; the conversation is never one-sided. Think of this as a conversation with yourself and your inner world. If you get a reversed card that you dislike, don't be afraid to work with it and explore how to shift your take on it in your readings. Consider what it means for it to become upright again, what you need to do in order to remove the blockage or create balance. When you change it to its upright position with your hands, feel whatever is represented by that spread position flow more openly and correct itself. This is the power of ritual and symbolic action – to trust that a movement of your hands also shapes the outline of your life.

READING TAROT

Reading the tarot involves a combination of using your conscious desire to search for truth, meaning, and purpose alongside your ability to listen to and interpret the voice of your unconscious, which finds its mirror image in the cards. In the following pages, you'll uncover the patterns and the structure behind the tarot, giving you a holistic and overarching vision of the self. You'll discover ways to develop your ability to connect with your unconscious through readings you conduct for both yourself and others. We'll also explore a number of spread types that you can use in your readings to gain insight into specific issues or seek guidance on different aspects of your life.

THE ANATOMY OF THE DECK

Standard tarot decks consist of 78 cards; 22 Major Arcana and 56 Minor Arcana. Understanding how the deck is structured is the key to finding order and clarity within the cards. They are not just 78 random archetypes – they exist within a strong web of relationships.

THE MAJOR ARCANA

The first 22 cards of your tarot deck are known as the Major Arcana. These cards represent larger life lessons that come together to form something called the Fool's Journey.

The Fool's Journey describes the path of the soul from innocence to individuation. It represents the universal search for personal growth and meaning. Every one of us is the Fool on our own journey; and though each path is as unique as the individual that walks it, they all comprise universal elements. The Fool's Journey can be further broken down into three stages, or in occult terminology, septenaries. We exclude the Fool, who represents the person taking the journey. Many teachers have given these stages different names, but all have several characteristics in common. They can be understood sequentially, or as different layers of the journey itself. These stages of the journey fall into three categories: The Conscious (cards 1-7); The Unconscious (cards 8-14); and The Superconscious (cards 15-21).

THE CONSCIOUS

body · social · external · outer concerns
youth · personal

1 **The Magician** 2 **The High Priestess**
3 **The Empress** 4 **The Emperor**
5 **The Hierophant** 6 **The Lovers**
7 **The Chariot**

This stage looks at material concerns that affect our worldly lives. Imagine a child being born into the world, discovering their will, meeting their parents, confronting others, and developing their ego. This can describe the process of growing into adulthood.

The Magician

THE UNCONSCIOUS

mind · moral · internal · inward search
adulthood · collective

8 **Strength**   9 **The Hermit**
10 **Wheel of Fortune**   11 **Justice**
12 **The Hanged Man**   13 **Death**
14 **Temperance**

The focus here is on one's inner world, and
the search for identity. We confront many
aspects and facets of the self, as well as
challenges and decisions that will help define
who we are. Thus, many of the themes in
this stage are moral.

THE SUPERCONSCIOUS

emotional · hidden · maturity · divine
universal · spiritual awareness

15 **The Devil**   16 **The Tower**
17 **The Star**   18 **The Moon**
19 **The Sun**   20 **Judgment**
21 **The World**

This final section deals with the Fool's
experiences as they develop awareness of
their role and place within the greater
universe. Here we learn to connect with the
eternal and universal forces of
the psyche.

Strength

The Devil

THE MINOR ARCANA & NUMEROLOGY

The Minor Arcana consists of the remainder of the deck – all the suit cards, including the court cards. They generally concern mundane matters in the course of one's life (from the Ace to 10), aspects of the self, or literal people in one's life (the court cards).

With some awareness of the elements, numerology, and the court card roles, we can combine those meanings in order to arrive at an overarching understanding of the Minor Arcana cards. This can be helpful for those new to reading tarot, as well as for more experienced readers to obtain multiple layers of meaning with each tarot reading.

Using cups as our example, the following Minor cards can serve as a reference for numerological meanings that will aid you in obtaining a quick understanding of the Ace to 10.

ACE	TWO

individuality	duality
beginnings	choices
potential	balance
momentum	cooperation
inspiration	

SIX	SEVEN

harmony	introspection
adjustment	investigation
alignment	reflection
commitment	spirituality
pleasure	

THREE

groups
raw energy
development
expression
creativity

FOUR

structure
manifestation
foundations
stability
endurance

FIVE

conflict
fluctuation
change
challenges

EIGHT

achievement
rebirth
perfection
action

NINE

attainment
nearing completion
abundance
idealism

TEN

completion
fulfilment
success
full circle

THE SUITS & THE ELEMENTS

Each of the suits in a tarot deck – wands, cups, swords, and pentacles – corresponds with an element and its overarching themes, so some knowledge of the elements and what they represent can be a helpful shortcut to understanding a large group of cards.

WANDS | FIRE

willpower · creativity · passion
inspiration · energy

Natural occurrences of the fire element in the world include explosive volcanoes, and blazing fires that are both destructive and purifying. Fire brings light in darkness, and warmth in cold. The wands represent the first spark of life within humanity – giving energy to create, as well as the passion and willpower to sustain creation.

Ace of Wands

CUPS | WATER

emotions · intuition · instincts
relationships · love

Cups represent the life-giving element of water. We drink from them to replenish us, so this suit is associated with healing. But water also has mysterious depths, like our emotions; they can be as gentle as a stream, or as forceful as a tidal wave. Water is adaptable, changing its form as it needs to, alluding to its resilience but also reactivity.

Two of Cups

SWORDS | AIR

ideas · thoughts
communications · conflict

Like the air, our thoughts are invisible, swift, and in flux. The air carries messages, so we associate it with communication. When we focus our thoughts and intellect, they become like swords. They can be cutting, penetrating, and sharp, like a frosty gust of wind that cuts to the core, or a harsh string of words.

Five of Swords

PENTACLES | EARTH

material world · nature · resources
finances · health

The earth is tangible; we can hold it in our hands. It is connected with the material world, nature, and even our bodily health. The pentacles represent the earth, for its stability, nourishment, and fertility allows things to flourish. It symbolizes our resources; finances, property, business, and possessions.

Page of Pentacles

THE COURT CARDS

The court cards are based on universal archetypes, whose reflections we can see within the family unit. We can further categorize these roles into different polarities, and an associated action and event. Though we use terminology associated with gender, the roles here are gender-fluid.

PAGES | CHILDREN

Focus Internal **Events** Messages
Actions Learn

Imagine a child just discovering one of the elements; they are inexperienced, but curious. Their role is to be an observer and a student, trying to decipher messages and learn as much as they can in order to understand their suit.

Page of Swords

KNIGHTS | ADOLESCENTS

Focus External **Events** Movements
Actions Act

The knights are the rowdy teenagers of the family, eager to prove their worth and make their mark on the world. They are brave and passionate but sometimes go overboard. Their role is to move forward and turn their suit into action.

Knight of Cups

QUEENS | MOTHERS

Focus Internal **Events** Creativity
Actions Develop

Queens are mothers of their suit, more spiritually connected than their less mature counterparts. Their role is to develop and nurture the elements of their suit, both within as well as alongside others. They are the creators of their suit, and express its powers.

Queen of Wands

KINGS | FATHERS

Focus External **Events** Authority
Actions Control

The kings are the fathers – authority figures who are in high positions of power. Their role is to create order and structure, develop and enforce boundaries, and protect their suit. They are there to control the elements of their suit.

King of Pentacles

REVERSALS

Some tarot readers choose not to use reversals. If you find yourself avoiding reversals because you fear negative cards, here are some tips on how you can interpret them in a healthier way. Ideally, we can learn not to avoid perceived negativity, but face these cards with openness and courage.

LIGHT AND SHADOW

Avoid thinking of the cards in dualistic terms. Remember that each card is an archetype, and it holds both a light and a shadow. When we separate these sides, as human nature loves to do, something is forgotten and repressed. Seemingly positive cards can become disastrous if there is too much of a good thing – for example, too much of The Sun's positivity can make us overlook faults, or areas where we can improve.

SYMBOLS NOT OMENS

When we avoid thinking of the cards as telling one's future, but rather see them as a tool that gives our inner world a voice, much of the fear dissipates. We can understand the Five of Pentacles not as "you'll be poor", but perhaps as a message that you feel impoverished, deprived, and that you're struggling. This may or may not correlate with actual material circumstances. The cards can help you to practise thinking about things in a symbolic way.

A LARGER STORY

Think of the Fool's Journey, and remember that each card is part of a larger tale. After the destruction in the tower, there is life. After the immense suffering in the Three of Swords, there is healing and rejuvenation in the Four. The wheel always turns.

REFRAME NEGATIVE CARDS

This goes hand-in-hand with learning to be more positive and resilient in general. Consider card reversals as an opportunity to find areas of improvement. The Tower is experienced as a collapse of foundations, but it is also the card of breakthroughs and of destroying illusions or outdated beliefs.

WHICH INTERPRETATION?

We can derive the reversal meaning from the original card in a few different ways. Knowing which interpretation to use can be tricky. You'll have to use your storytelling abilities, your intuition, and the reading's context to better understand which meanings are applicable. It is important to note that different methods of reversal interpretation can sometimes give the same results.

Let's take the **Knight of Wands** as our example card to explore the different methods that could be applied. Upright, the Knight of Wands is bold, adventurous, and brave – this person is enterprising, enthusiastic, and always expanding their horizons. But they know their limits. In reverse, four different meanings could be applicable: there could be too much of the original energy at play, or not enough. Alternatively there could be a blockage of the upright energy, or the opposite energy could be signalled (see right).

1. EXCESS OF ORIGINAL ENERGY

When the original energy of the card becomes too much, this Knight can be reckless, forceful, volatile, and unreliable. This person can't be counted on, their moods are fickle, and they don't care about consequences or others.

2. DECREASE OF ORIGINAL ENERGY

When the original energy of the card dissipates too much this person may be cautious, careful, and hesitant. Without this card's upright energy, they are more considerate, and therefore more wary of their actions.

3. BLOCKED ENERGY

When there is an obstacle to fully expressing the original energy of the card, this person can be responsible and beholden. They may want to take risks and explore, but might have many duties they can't escape.

4. THE OPPOSITE ENERGY

This is the simplest interpretation and all of the above reasons can lead to the opposite meaning being derived. Someone who displays the opposite of this Knight's upright energy may be timid, fearful, or docile. This person may show signs of cowardice.

The Knight of Wands reversed

HOW TO READ THE CARDS

Now that you're equipped with a basic understanding of the tarot deck's structure, the following steps will guide you through your tarot readings, from choosing a spread and phrasing questions to interpreting the story of the cards.

1 | CHOOSE A SPREAD

The tarot spreads are layouts and configurations for tarot cards that form the structure of your reading. They can probe specific aspects of one's life, like relationship spreads, but can also be more general to give you a comprehensive overview of your current situation.

A spread consists of positions, which are representative of one specific facet of your reading. You may want answers to why a relationship is going sour; but that usually consists of many variables, such as your role in the problem, the other person's role in the problem, external factors, and what each of you can do to mend it. Each of these facets is potentially represented by a position. A tarot spread is essentially a way of breaking down a problem into its components. See pages 28-39 for a selection of tarot spreads that you can use or customize for your own purposes.

2 | CONSIDER HOW TO PHRASE QUESTIONS

To deliver a satisfying tarot reading it is essential to ask the right kinds of questions. It can be the difference between a reading that is illuminating, empowering, insightful, and productive – versus one that is simply about confirming biases, fears, and reinforcing one's feeling of powerlessness. Your questions should always be:

OPEN ENDED

Tarot is a medium that doesn't like being asked *"what"*, but rather *"why"*. Take advantage of that strength. You may be tempted to ask questions that require a simple yes or no answer, but there are often too many factors at play to obtain a simplistic answer like this.

For example: Instead of asking *"Will I get the job?"* ask *"What can I do to increase my chances of getting the job?"* Rather than asking *"Does he love me?"* try *"How can we improve our relationship?"*

FOCUSED ON THE SEEKER

When our readings involve others, it can be tempting to use the tarot to give us an insight into their mental state or feelings. This can be false comfort; giving us a sense of control over others that doesn't really exist.

For example: Don't ask *"What does my boss think about me?"* rather try asking *"How can I get more respect at work?"* Rather than asking *"Does my ex still love me?"* instead ask *"Is my relationship with my ex worth saving?"*

FOCUSED ON TAKING ACTION

Even when we feel trapped in a corner, there are ways of approaching problems that can make a real difference. Choosing to dwell on what you can't do to change a situation, instead of what you can, takes away your sense of agency.

For example: Instead of asking *"Will I ever be happy?"* ask *"What can I do to improve my circumstances?"* Rather than asking *"Will I win the lottery?"* try *"How can I work on improving my financial situation?"*

FOCUSED ON THE PRESENT

Though tarot's reputation lends it to be perceived as a fortune-telling method, we need to remember that our future is not predetermined. Focus on the journey of creating the future – of actively shaping it, instead of trying to divine a predestined fate. Focusing on the past, too, and wondering what could have been is likely to lead to dead ends.

For example: Don't ask *"Was it right to leave my job for this new position?"* instead try asking *"What is missing from my current job?"* Rather than asking *"How will the wedding turn out?"* ask *"What do I need to consider about the wedding?"*

3 SHUFFLE THE CARDS

Shuffling the cards clears and resets the deck. You may prefer not to shuffle them like playing cards and instead take small stacks from the middle of the deck, and place them on top. This can be done many times, until the cards are sufficiently randomized and your mind is still.

As you engage in the repetitive motion of shuffling the cards, feel your mind clear. Focus on how the cards feel as they pass through your hands. When we learn to master a repetitive action to the point where it becomes almost automatic, another part of our mind can surface.

4 SET YOUR INTENTION

You don't have to do this out loud, but hearing yourself speak can have a powerful impact. This can come in the form of asking your question, a short prayer, an invocation, or a personal mantra.

5 DRAW THE CARDS

You can now either fan the cards out on a smooth surface to draw them, or just draw the cards directly from the top of the deck.

As you draw each of the cards, describe what you see in them as if describing them to another person. This helps us notice more details than when we view the images passively. More things may stand out to you when using this method. Don't try to look up meanings, or remember them now; focus on what you see. Place them in your chosen spread formation.

6 RELATE EACH CARD TO THE SPREAD POSITION

Consider what is being asked at this position and how it relates to the question. If you need to, look up the card meanings (see pages 42–217). Can you create a narrative or story?

For example: The card is the Three of Cups, the position is "past", and the question is about finding love. Consider how past friendships have shaped your stance on love. Have previous relationships started as friendships? Were your friends ever disapproving of past relationships?

7 | LOOK AT THE WHOLE PICTURE

Once you've drawn everything, search for larger patterns. Look out for the following:

• **Ratio of Major to Minor Arcana** An abundance of Major Arcana could indicate that there are many life lessons related to the reading, giving it weight and importance.

• **Ratio of suits** A dominance of one suit can signal the importance of the corresponding element. Many cups cards, for example, can indicate that relationships and one's emotional state play a strong role.

• **Ratio of reversals** A high ratio of reversals can signal lots of blocked energy, or extremist thinking.

• **Ratio of court cards** A lot of these can indicate many external influences.

• **What is missing?** This can signal something being overlooked. If you're doing a reading about finances, for example, but there are no pentacles cards, it can indicate an impractical approach that needs to be more grounded in reality.

8 | CLOSE THE READING

Reunite your cards, and shuffle again. You may also like to give thanks to your cards for their guidance.

THREE-CARD SPREADS

Many tarot spreads are complex and geared towards exploring a particular problem. But some days our lives are simpler, which is where these spreads come in. The following spreads are easy and short enough to do every day, to check in on a recurring issue, or to form the foundation of a daily tarot practice.

DAILY CHECK-IN

These are best used for when you don't have a specific problem, but as a simple method of self-care, introspection, and bringing ritual into your life.

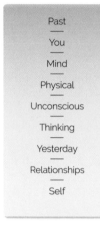

CARD 1	CARD 2	CARD 3
Past	Present	Future
You	Relationship	Partner
Mind	Body	Spirit
Physical	Emotional	Spiritual
Unconscious	Conscious	Superconscious
Thinking	Feeling	Doing
Yesterday	Today	Tomorrow
Relationships	Work	Play
Self	Other	Purpose

DECISION MAKING

These spreads help you clarify your position on decisions that you need to make, and the factors involved in your choices.

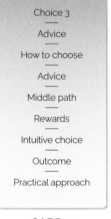

CARD 1	CARD 2	CARD 3
Choice 1	Choice 2	Choice 3
Strengths	Weaknesses	Advice
Choice 1	Choice 2	How to choose
Situation	Obstacle	Advice
Good	Evil	Middle path
Action	Consequences	Rewards
Logical choice	Emotional choice	Intuitive choice
Action	Reaction	Outcome
Optimistic approach	Pessimistic approach	Practical approach

GUIDANCE AND EVALUATIONS

Our daily lives can be filled with uncertainty; These spreads are intended to analyse a situation by breaking it down into distinct components, revealing truths, and dispelling confusion.

CARD 1	CARD 2	CARD 3
What worked	What didn't work	Lessons
Brings together	Pulls apart	Focus
Opportunities	Difficulties	Advice
Divine feminine	Divine masculine	Inner child
Best-case scenario	Worst-case scenario	Likely outcome
External challenge	Internal challenge	Potential
Emotion	Emotion's source	Advice
Fear	Your response	Better response
Your perspective	Their perspective	Outsider perspective
Needs	Desires	Fears
Your passion	Your imagination	Your logic

GOAL PROGRESS

These spreads are suitable for simple daily check-ins on your progress when you have a specific goal in mind.

CARD 1	CARD 2	CARD 3
You	Your position	Your potential
Idea	Process	Goal
Goal	Challenge	Overcoming challenge
Desire	Conflict	Resolution
Passion	Direction	Destination

CLASSIC SPREADS

Classic spreads can be thought of as "general" tarot spreads, as they are intended to explore and tackle many different problems. They are also ideal when we don't have a particular question, or are looking to understand life from a wider perspective. Below are two classics that are particularly powerful.

CELTIC CROSS

The Celtic Cross can be applied to any situation that needs a deeper level of insight. It's popular for a reason; it is flexible, can be used with or without a question, and simplifies many complex, convoluted issues into digestible pieces.

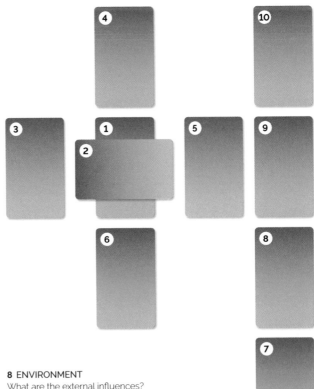

1 HEART OF THE MATTER
What is currently happening? What is the querent's situation or emotional state?

2 CHALLENGE
What stands in your way? What needs to be resolved?

3 PAST
What past events are shaping the current situation?

4 CONSCIOUS
Where is your mind? What are your assumptions? What is your focus?

5 FUTURE
What is likely to happen if nothing changes? What are the short-term possibilities?

6 UNCONSCIOUS
What truly drives this situation? What hidden factors are its foundations?

7 QUERENT
What is the querent's view of this? How does that affect the situation?

8 ENVIRONMENT
What are the external influences? What is the social environment surrounding this situation?

9 HOPES AND FEARS
What do you secretly desire? Or what are you trying to avoid?

10 OUTCOME
Given the rest of the spread, what is the likely resolution? Summary, theme, or advice.

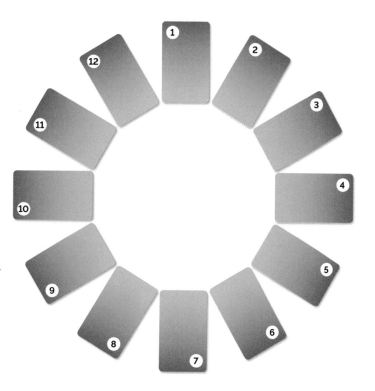

ZODIAC

This popular spread type is inspired by astrology. By assigning a card position to each part of the zodiac wheel and the houses, we have a spread that is great for in-depth check-ins. You can use a zodiac spread monthly or quarterly as a means of getting insight, clarity, and advice on different areas of your life, from work to relationships. You can then consider what you will need to adjust going forward.

1 ARIES | IDENTITY
How are you viewing yourself at the moment? What first impressions do you give to others?

2 TAURUS | VALUE
What is your material situation? How are you relating to your resources?

3 GEMINI | COMMUNICATION
Is your communication clear? Are there misunderstandings that you can correct?

4 CANCER | HOME
How is your family and home life? What emotions do you need to address here?

5 LEO | CREATIVITY
How are you expressing yourself creatively? Can you make more time in your life for playfulness?

6 VIRGO | HEALTH AND ROUTINES
What is your daily routine? How are you addressing your health during this period?

7 LIBRA | RELATIONSHIPS
What is your romantic life like at the moment?

8 SCORPIO | TRANSFORMATION
What changes have occurred during this season? Where is there intensity in your life right now?

9 SAGITTARIUS | PHILOSOPHY
What in your life is particularly meaningful? What belief system is inspiring you or driving your actions?

10 CAPRICORN | AMBITION
What are your aspirations? What are you working towards? What is your reputation and your status?

11 AQUARIUS | COMMUNITY
What are your friendships bringing you right now? How are you working within the context of larger groups?

12 PISCES | INNER LIFE
What is happening in your inner world? Are there anxieties, secrets, dreams, hopes, and desires?

RELATIONSHIP SPREADS

Relationships, whether romantic in nature or otherwise, are common topics for a tarot reading. The following spreads focus on two aspects of relationships: developing bonds, and what to do during conflict. They are designed to help explore emotional connections and work through specific issues.

DYNAMICS

Whether it's about romantic compatibility, or just understanding how well partners get along, this tarot spread examines the relationship, and what is needed to create a strong emotional bond between two people.

1 YOU
How do you see yourself in this particular relationship?

2 OTHER
How do you see your partner in this particular relationship?

3 RELATIONSHIP
How do you view the relationship in its current state?

4 EXPECTATIONS
What do you want and expect from this relationship? What is most important to you?

5 STRENGTHS
How does this relationship make you both stronger?

6 WEAKNESSES
What challenges does this relationship present? How does this relationship hurt you both?

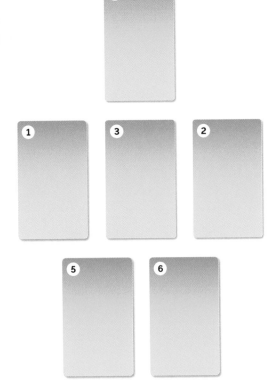

CONFLICT RESOLUTION

When relationships go sour, this spread is intended to evaluate different aspects of how it happened, why, and whether the relationship can – or should – be healed.

1 YOUR ROLE
How did you contribute to the conflict? How did you let it escalate?

2 THEIR ROLE
How did they contribute to the conflict? How did they escalate it?

3 EXTERNAL FACTORS
What influences outside the relationship contributed to this particular conflict?

4 WHAT TO IMPROVE
What can you do better to help heal and improve this relationship?

5 WHAT TO AVOID
What behaviours do you need to curb? What do you do that makes this conflict worse?

6 LESSON
What lessons can now be learned from this conflict?

7 IS RESOLUTION WORTH IT?
Is this relationship worth saving? Will you both find happiness here?

8 ADVICE
Given the whole picture, what should you do now?

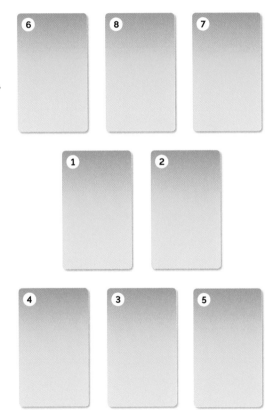

WORK SPREADS

Questions concerning work and career frequently arise during readings, usually in times of transition. These examples will enable you to examine your current path, or evaluate a new one. They will help you to analyse your goals and assess whether the time is right to move on.

CAREER REFLECTION

This is a spread to use when looking for more clarity on work and career matters. It can be used when at a crossroads, or if you're feeling stuck, or even for a simple monthly checkup on your career goals.

1 PURPOSE
What drives you in this job? What gives you purpose?

2 RESPONSIBILITIES
What are your responsibilities, and how do you feel about them?

3 TALENTS
Where do your talents, skills, and abilities lie?

4 RESOURCES
What resources do you have that can aid you in your growth?

5 TO FIX
What in your current position needs to be fixed?

6 TO RELEASE
What needs to be removed, released, or let go?

7 TO REFLECT
What else do you need to consider? What do you need answers for?

8 REWARDS
What do you hope to gain from your work life or career? What is your ideal outcome?

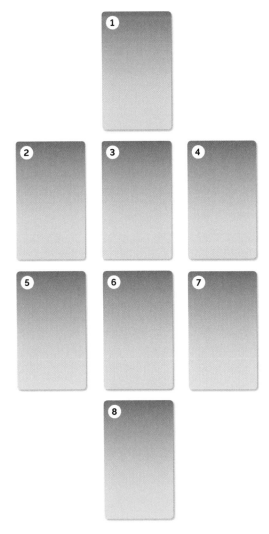

NEW VENTURE

If you are setting out on a new work-related journey, such as setting up a business or starting a new job, you can use this spread to help you prepare and plan your future.

1 MOTIVATION
Why do you want to start this business or take on this new role?

2 CHALLENGES
What will be your biggest obstacle in setting out on this venture?

3 EMOTIONAL GOAL
What do you hope to gain from this venture emotionally? What do you hope to learn?

4 PRACTICAL GOAL
What do you hope to gain materially? What rewards do you seek?

5 WHAT YOU OFFER
What talents and skills can you offer potential clients or customers?

6 WHAT MAKES YOU SPECIAL
How do you differentiate yourself from competitors?

7 ROUTINE
What does your routine at this venture look like day to day?

8 POTENTIAL
What are your clients missing? What gap can you fill?

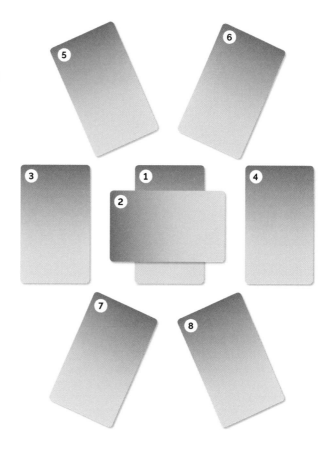

SPIRITUAL SPREADS

These spiritual tarot spreads are all about helping you with internal work; they are designed to enable you to connect with your inner voice, develop a better understanding of yourself and your core emotions, and forge a closer relationship with your subconscious.

DREAM INTERPRETATION

Our dreams are a window into our unconscious and, like the tarot, they often present themselves in symbols and imagery. Sometimes, this imagery is obscure and difficult to understand, but incredibly powerful. This spread can be useful in presenting some answers.

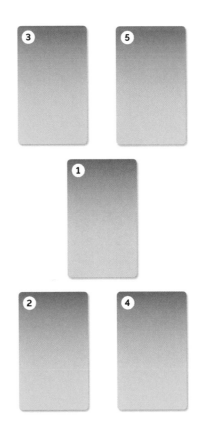

1 DREAMER
What is your role in the dream? What part do you play?

2 THEME
What is the main message conveyed by this dream?

3 CONNECTED EVENT
What in your waking life is this dream speaking to? What part of your waking life caused this dream?

4 WHAT IS REPRESSED
What feelings or thoughts have you not consciously integrated, and are now appearing in your dreams?

5 LESSON
What do you need to learn from this dream in your waking life? What should you do?

SELF-CARE

Sometimes, all we need is a way to check in with our emotions. This self-care spread is designed to help you do just that, as well as present you with some guidance on how you can better take care of yourself.

1 YOUR FEELINGS NOW
How are you right now? What is your current emotional state?

2 SOOTHE
What can you do now to tend to and heal yourself?

3 ACCEPT
What are you repressing that you must accept in order to be able to move forward?

4 ADAPT
What in your life needs to change? What aspects have you been stubborn about?

5 WITHDRAW
What do you need to retreat from? What should you now distance yourself from?

6 EMBRACE
What can you learn to accept more lovingly? What can be integrated and welcomed into your life?

7 CELEBRATE
What aspects, accomplishments, events, or milestones in your life can you be grateful for?

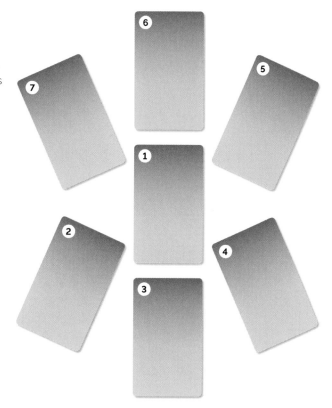

CREATING YOUR OWN SPREAD

Designing your own tarot spread is a great exercise in creative problem solving, as well as a way to develop a greater bond with your tarot cards. Making a bespoke spread enables you to tailor it exactly to your needs. Follow these steps whenever you have a question with no seemingly matching spread.

1 | UNDERSTAND YOUR PURPOSE

While the question may be obvious, it takes a little bit of self-knowledge, or empathy, to truly understand your goal or that of the seeker. There may be longer-term, unspoken desires at play here. Try and get a sense of these before the reading begins.

Example: Hannah feels unfulfilled in her relationship and has had a string of arguments over small things with her partner. She is asking if they should break up. The goal of the reading here can really be: How can Hannah have a more fulfilling romantic life? Should that be with this partner or another?

2 | CREATE POSITIONS

Reading the tarot is really about crafting stories, and every story has the following:

Context
Problem
Solution

This can be a three-card spread in itself. But we can tailor more questions based on these three components. Each question turns into a position.

Creating questions is really about working out what you need to know to obtain a helpful answer. Each question should always be about empowering yourself or the seeker (see pages 24-25).

Example: Now to create a few positions for each of the categories arising from Hannah's specific goal and questions from step 1. They will be:

1 **Context** How do Hannah's past relationships affect her perception of romance?
2 **Context** How are Hannah's emotions in general?
3 **Context** What does Hannah expect from love?
4 **Problem** What is missing from her romance?
5 **Problem** What stands between her and her partner?
6 **Solution** How can she overcome these challenges in her current relationship?
7 **Solution** General advice for Hannah's love life.

3 | ORDER AND LAYOUT

Once you have the positions, you'll need to name these and arrange them in an order that makes sense, and best tells the story. This will be the order in which you draw the cards from the deck.

Create a visual layout; your spread formation – this is optional, but can be helpful in organizing one's mental understanding of the cards. Symmetry can help in understanding opposing sides of the problem – weaknesses versus strengths, conscious versus unconscious, for example. Being on the left or right is a good way to show time progression. Having a central focus also helps.

Example: Hannah is at the centre. She is surrounded by changes in the past (4 and 6) and future (5 and 7), and is contrasting expectations (2) versus reality (3).

1 Emotional environment How are Hannah's emotions in general right now?
2 Assumptions What does Hannah expect from love?
3 Unfulfilled need What is missing from her romance?
4 Obstacle What stands between her and her partner?
5 Solution How can she overcome these challenges in her current relationship?
6 Past relationships How do past relationships affect her perception of romance?
7 Advice General advice for Hannah's love life.

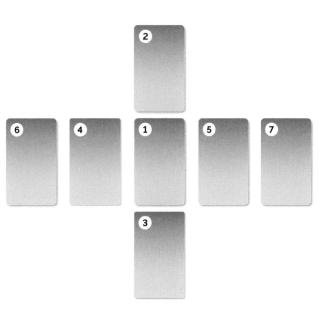

THE MAJOR ARCANA

The Major Arcana comprises the universal spiritual path that every human takes from unaware innocence to self-actualization. This is called the Fool's Journey, which is also our collective, but uniquely individual path through life. This journey encompasses people you will meet, archetypes that you will become, decisions that shape who you are, and forces that connect you with the universe. Although the cards depict varying manifestations of the human form, all the figures are meant to represent you and your higher self.

THE FOOL

UPRIGHT		REVERSE
potential · new beginnings		unprepared · careless
freedom · innocence		immature · reckless
blank slate · optimism		hesitant · apprehensive

UPRIGHT

REVERSE

Interpretation

The upright Fool is representative of the infinite potential that we all have within us. She is the source of primal energy – innocent and free, a blank slate that later becomes moulded as she undertakes the path of self-knowledge. She throws her heart into adventure, without fear. The Fool can signal the start of a new path – one that is full of risks, but also great rewards.

In reverse, the Fool's enthusiasm and naivety can become rash and hasty. She may also be blind to how her missteps may be affecting others, choosing not to see or accept the consequences of her actions. On the other hand, the reversed Fool may signal hesitation and doubt. The fearlessness that is usually present in the Fool is now absent – all that she sees are potentials for mistakes.

Reflection

You may be yearning for new beginnings and adventures into the unknown. What would you do if nothing stood in your way? Have you been given a chance to experience a new world – whether in the form of a change in career, an exciting new romance, or a trip to a new country? The Fool's optimism will serve you well during these voyages.

New journeys – whether they concern relationships, creative ventures, or career moves – can inspire complex emotions. Are you so enthusiastic that you are not considering the bigger picture: how do your choices fit into the framework of your life? Or are you out of your comfort zone and fearful of what you will have to sacrifice?

Action

Be curious Tap into your sense of adventure, wonder, and curiosity. Opportunities are available everywhere, as long as you have the eyes and inclination to look for them.

Explore new territories Consider what new experiences are awaiting you that you haven't yet embraced because of fear. Now is a good time to try new things.

Let go of expectations Perhaps you play into expectations that are not aligned with who you want to be and your highest potential. It may be as simple as changing your style, or as complex as a career change.

Address your fears Think about what it is that is holding you back from taking the next big step in your life. When we don't confront what scares us, it means that these fears remain in the dark, lurking and festering. By shining a light onto them, you may start to see that they are not necessarily the huge obstacles you have built them up to be.

Confront unknowns Sometimes the best thing to do when taking that first step is to know what you don't know. Once you know your blind spots, research and learn as much as you can to prevent future mistakes.

THE MAGICIAN

UPRIGHT	REVERSE
power · skill · manifestation	scattered · directionless
concentration · creation	distracted · trickster
will · intention	illusions · charlatan

UPRIGHT

REVERSE

Interpretation

When the Fool becomes the Magician, he realizes that he has profound agency in the path that he is taking – that it can shift and undulate according to his will. In this way, the Magician is the embodiment of willpower, choice, and desire. He is the key to all magic, and a reminder that intention and perspective can be great tools to manifest tangible outcomes.

The Magician may sometimes use his great power for unscrupulous reasons, weaving illusions, tricks, and deceptions for his own gain. Healthy ambition can become ruthless manipulation. On the other hand, the absence of the Magician's fundamental forces can indicate a lack of clarity. Without his desire, he may be unfocused, having no particular place to devote his energy.

Reflection

When you look within and acknowledge your power, you will learn that creating your own fate is not only possible, but is your responsibility alone. What can you do right now to set your goals into motion? What changes do you have to make? You can create the world you want to see, and that starts with yourself.

Stop and take a moment to remember the foundations of your desire. As you lose focus are you tending to do things that are not aligned with your values and principles? Are you misusing your talents when you are blinded by your aspirations? Get back in touch with your true desires for they will lead you to where you need to go.

Action

Channel your desires Envisage your ideal path forward, and imagine what it would feel like if it were a reality. Contemplate those dreams to breathe life into that vision.

Know your power Understand the internal traits that can help you create your world; write down any natural strengths and abilities that may enable you to realize your vision.

Acknowledge your tools Consider your external environment and the resources available to you. These could be material, financial, or come in the form of relationships with people who can help you.

Remember your purpose Reminding yourself of why you do what you do can help bring clarity and direction as you re-align with your best self. Perhaps you had to make compromises along the way. You could be making career or life decisions now that don't serve your true purpose, so get back in touch with your original intentions.

Simplify your approach When you know what you want, you can begin clearing away distractions. If you are trying to do too many things, consider the tasks you can let go of that won't detract from your overall goal.

THE HIGH PRIESTESS

UPRIGHT	**REVERSE**
intuition · unconscious	repression · superficiality
spirituality · stillness	ignoring intuition
mystery · dreams	repressed · disconnected

UPRIGHT

REVERSE

Interpretation

The High Priestess represents our relationship with our inner world. She is our faculty of intuition and divine wisdom; she is the voice that calls out from the depths, equipped with knowledge of all that is hidden: our true natures, spirituality, and the self. Her task is to teach us how we can illuminate our dreams, fantasies, and fears with the light of awareness.

When the High Priestess is reversed, the messages she relays from your inner self are not being received or understood. Her voice is being drowned out by external inputs: anxieties, the wishes and opinions of others, overthinking, societal expectations, guilt, or even past traumas. Perhaps over time, as these other issues have taken precedence, her voice, too, has grown weaker and weaker.

Reflection

The answers you seek can be found within. Amongst the bustle of everyday life, there is a peaceful core that unflinchingly knows your inner truth. This wisdom is your compass. What is your intuition trying to tell you? If conventional methods of problem solving are not working for your creative, professional, or personal projects, what does your gut say?

Do you feel disconnected with your self? Have you developed behaviours, attitudes, or coping mechanisms that are not aligned with your highest potential? Are you operating on autopilot? Perhaps you are repressing the voice that is telling you a change needs to be made. It is now that you need the High Priestess's wisdom more than ever.

Action

Label the sensation Be mindful of moments when your intuition is calling out to you. What does it feel like in your body? It may come in the form of warmth in your gut or chest, or a sharp sense of clarity.

Explore your unconscious Keep a dream journal. Understanding patterns and common symbols in your dreams can be a helpful starting point for developing a deeper connection to your inner self.

Follow your intuition Make decisions based on your intuition, and take note of what happens both emotionally and externally.

Slow down Pause and give yourself some time to relax. Life may seem like an endless to-do list, but without also devoting some time alone to introspect and recharge, our connection to ourselves grows weaker. Cultivating stillness can also help process the inputs you receive from the world.

Unravel external voices Where are all the "should"s coming from? Sometimes they are so ingrained in us, that they become internalized. Learning to distinguish between all these voices can help us find the thread that leads to our own self.

THE EMPRESS

UPRIGHT

creativity · abundance
nature · fertility
feminine energy · nurturing

REVERSE

stagnation · scarcity
neglect · smothering
co-dependence

UPRIGHT

REVERSE

Interpretation

The Empress is the embodiment of the divine feminine energy that is deeply creative, expressive, and sensual. She is tied to the earthly realm and the delights of the senses, with an innate connection to the natural world. Her state of abundance is coupled with a maternal instinct, one that is nurturing and compassionate, but also fiercely protective of all that is vulnerable and sacred.

When the Empress is reversed, the flow of her creative energy can be blocked. Her abundance has turned into a feeling of scarcity. On the other hand, it can indicate that her usual nurturing character may have gone overboard. When she focuses too much on the needs of others at the expense of herself, her care can become meddling, overprotective, controlling, and smothering.

Reflection

What can you show gratitude for – the peaceful sway of trees in the wind, or the sun's rays on a cold morning? Could the beauty in these moments inspire you to start a new project? Appreciation and connection with all that surrounds us also develops our sense of empathy. Do you feel the need to care for others? How can you support them?

Are you experiencing stagnation in your creative efforts at the moment? Abundance, and knowing that the world provides for you in all circumstances, creates confidence and inspires. When we feel lacking in resources, our creativity can be blocked. Are you spending your resources on others, when you need to focus them on yourself?

Action

Take pleasure in your senses See, hear, taste, touch, and smell everything. Notice the little details that can sometimes pass you by. When we are more in touch with our sensuality, we can also more deeply appreciate our natural world.

Start a creative project Take advantage of your newly heightened creative energy – ideas come more easily to you now.

Venture into nature Whether gardening or taking a hike in the mountains, feeling connected with the natural world helps us feel more firmly rooted in our bodies.

Focus on self care It is not selfish to take care of yourself. You can't burn yourself to keep another person warm. Take a bubble bath, get a massage, anything that will help you recharge your batteries.

Change your environment Try to create a fresh space that feels comfortable. Curating your environment can be a way of cultivating the fertile ground of imagination in yourself.

Believe in your own abundance Remind yourself that you have all the resources you need to thrive within yourself. Focus on what you have, not on what you don't.

THE EMPEROR

UPRIGHT	**REVERSE**
authority · structure	tyranny · dictator
logic · masculine energy	callous · avoidant
protection · discipline	ineffective · entitled

UPRIGHT

REVERSE

Interpretation

The Emperor is our ability to structure, organize, protect, and create stability. He does this through developing rules and systems, fostering discipline, creating boundaries, honouring values, and ruling with authority. As such, he accomplishes all his tasks with a fearsome efficiency. He is also a protective figure, who is unafraid of conflict, and will defend his borders without hesitation.

The reversed Emperor can either be an ineffective leader or a ruthless tyrant. He may wilt at the call of actual duty, and at the next moment, rage at a snide comment made about his clothes. With such an incompetent king, others may vie for his crown, and he may be unable to stop them. He may instead make a big show of his dominance, abusing his authority and hurting many in the process.

Reflection

You may be surrounded by chaos, but harnessing your inner Emperor can help bring a sense of calm. How can you become more assertive and stand up for yourself, your values, and your beliefs, either at work or within relationships? What in your life needs organization and discipline? What areas could benefit from a firm hand?

Is there an overreach of power, either by you or someone in your life? What is your relationship to power or authority? Do you distrust it? Do you crave it? Sometimes we need to protect our boundaries, but we may believe that taking a stand can be too aggressive. Do you say "yes" when you mean "no"? This can damage your sense of self.

Action

Create structure and process Rules and methodologies can be helpful in getting things done without emotional baggage clouding the view. If there is chaos at work, develop a project outline with responsibilities, roles, and duties.

Get disciplined When it comes to reaching your goals, try to take a step-by-step approach. Break the big picture down into smaller targets that are attainable with daily effort. For example, if you want to finish writing that novel, commit yourself to writing a small amount every day.

Say what you mean If you've been fed up about something, but keeping quiet for the sake of retaining equanimity, now is the time to respectfully communicate that. Do not be afraid to voice your feelings.

Establish boundaries The Emperor understands the importance of establishing strong borders around his territory. Without clear boundaries, you can signal to others that they are welcome to take control. Who or what will you allow in your territory? What is strictly not permitted? Establish your own set of boundaries and guard them.

THE HIEROPHANT

UPRIGHT

tradition · institution
education · social structures
hierarchical organizations

REVERSE

conformity · dogma
social pressure · restriction
conventionality

UPRIGHT

REVERSE

Interpretation

The Hierophant is a wise and respected teacher. He connects heaven and earth, and understands that in this complex game of life, everything has its role. From the tiniest bee to the great emperor himself, we all have our parts to play. Given this knowledge, it is natural for him to appreciate and uphold the social structures that keep everything in harmony and order.

When the Hierophant is reversed, the hierarchical structures that can create harmony and balance in our lives can instead become stale and ineffectual. A blind acceptance of the status quo could turn into the inability to accept change. Those who act as individuals may draw the judgment and ire of those who follow the rules; they can be shamed and pressured into falling in line.

Reflection

What can you learn from tradition? What uncertainties could you eliminate from your life by following a conventional path? This card also represents institutions and social structures. Being part of these groups can bring security and comfort. At this time, the desire to belong can be powerful. In what groups can you find a feeling of support?

As much as groups can provide comfort, they can also be merciless to those who do not fit their mould. Where are you feeling alienated, suppressed, or alone? Does your vision for what you want in life clash with what is "normal"? How can you break free from others' expectations? What could be possible if you choose to follow your own wisdom?

Action

Find a mentor When it comes to the tried and true methods, there's no better place to learn than from a mentor. Some guidance from someone with experience in your field can be helpful now.

Take a class Higher education falls under the realm of the Hierophant. A class can offer a way to expand the mind, as well as a chance to find camaraderie with classmates.

Honour tradition What traditions or rituals are important to you? Try to engage in one of these now, and observe how doing this offers you a sense of comfort.

Go your own way Don't accept things because "that's the way it is". Now is the time to stop following others and release yourself from narrow-minded dogma. You need to make some of your own rules. Shake off whatever is stifling you and vow to tread your own path.

Celebrate your individuality What quirky habits, talents, or characteristics do you have that you've been hiding for fear of judgment? Now you should be letting your guard down and expressing them. Learn to celebrate who you truly are.

THE LOVERS

UPRIGHT	**REVERSE**
love · relationships · union	imbalance · incompatibility
choices · commitment	disharmony · conflict
duality · lust	selfishness

UPRIGHT

REVERSE

Interpretation

The Lovers card represents pure, unconditional love. The relationship depicted here is one of trust, affection, and balance. Each complements and empowers the other, making the greater whole better than the sum of its parts. Alongside love, choices are also at the centre of this card. Each of the lovers makes a commitment and is choosing who they want to spend their life with.

When the Lovers are reversed, their relationship is no longer in harmony. Perhaps what was once a complementary partnership, where each party was different, but worked as a team to offset each other's weaknesses, now just feels like incompatibility. Reversed, the Lovers card points to a lack of choice and reflects the difficult decisions that we must make when there is no happy option.

Reflection

The Lovers card can refer to any strong relationship that you have in your life, or your relationship with yourself. Who makes you feel cherished, supported, and understood? This card can also refer to a pledge being made, such as the one the lovers are making to each other. What commitments should you be making to others or to yourself?

Reversed, this card suggests a close relationship being out of balance. Consider how much effort each person is putting into the relationship. Or perhaps this card is referring to an imbalance in your own psyche. Are you repressing or even shaming a side of your self? How can you use love to restore balance in yourself and with others?

Action

Analyse love In our lives we are bound to experience relationships that have both healthy and unhealthy dynamics. Think about your past relationships, and compare the ones that have felt controlling or stifling to those that were truly fulfilling. Consider how you can use these comparisons to help you assess your current situation, or find a healthy, happy relationship in the future.

Make a commitment There are times when we need to buckle down and make some decisions. Now you must make choices and take a firmer stance; commit to your path.

Rebalance the relationship Power dynamics can become unhealthy if one partner is more or less invested than the other. Consider how these imbalances affect you and your partner and what can be done to regain equilibrium in the partnership.

Develop self-love Instead of focusing on those parts of yourself that you are insecure about, those aspects that you don't like new lovers to see, work on improving your self-image. Write down all of your best attributes and the positive elements you bring to a relationship.

THE CHARIOT

UPRIGHT	REVERSE
determination · focus	unmotivated · distraction
grit · movement	narrow-mindedness
travel · direction	lack of control · fixation

UPRIGHT

REVERSE

Interpretation

At the core of the Chariot card is grit, perseverance, and focus. The Fool must now walk the path that he has determined for himself. He has learned from the Lovers about his two opposing natures, which now must work together to pull the Chariot forward. The charioteer must remain focused, take control of the situation, and ensure that he reaches his goal.

Reversed, the charioteer may be so focused on his goal that he either does not see how he has changed in his pursuit, or that there are alternatives that may give him similar outcomes without the stress. On the other hand, the charioteer may be experiencing diminished motivation or confidence, feeling overwhelmed and letting the opposing forces in his life take control.

Reflection

This card gives the impression of strong intent and willpower. When you have a goal in mind, but it seems difficult to reach, how do you deal with it? The Chariot asks you to call upon all your determination to see it through. The greatest victory is not whether or not you achieve that goal, but the journey that you take to accomplish it.

If you find yourself in pursuit of your goals to the detriment of enjoying life, now may be a good time to pause and reconsider the path you are travelling. What kinds of sacrifices are you making to achieve your dreams? You may also be feeling a sudden lack of resolve. Does this stem from fear, or more awareness of your shifting priorities?

Action

Take next steps Sometimes just doing that one extra task a day is enough to keep up the momentum. Even if it's something that seems trivial, all that work will add up over time.

Hold yourself accountable Whether it's keeping a list and sticking to it, or getting an accountability partner to help motivate you, use tools that will encourage you to stick to your goals.

Prioritize Work out what is absolutely necessary. Perhaps seemingly worthwhile tasks are distractions from your main goal.

Reassess your goal Consider if what you are pursuing is something that is still important to you now. Maybe there is a version of your goal that would allow you to feel the satisfaction of accomplishment without damaging other aspects of your life.

Identify distractions Think about where you are being pulled to, and why. Perhaps your change in direction reflects the desires of the ego rather than true self-knowledge.

Rethink your methods Consider alternative, easier paths. Perhaps you can take them without giving up your vision.

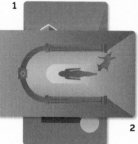

CELTIC CROSS

1 HEART OF THE MATTER
Emperor Reversed (see pp.50–51)

2 PROBLEM
Fool (see pp.42–43)

3 PAST
Ace of Swords (see pp.156–157)

4 CONSCIOUS
Temperance Reversed
(see pp.72–73)

5 FUTURE
Five of Pentacles (see pp.196–197)

6 UNCONSCIOUS
Three of Pentacles Reversed
(see pp.192–193)

7 QUERENT
Hermit (see pp.62–63)

8 ENVIRONMENT
Page of Wands (see pp.114–115)

9 HOPES AND FEARS
King of Pentacles Reversed
(see pp.216–217)

10 OUTCOME
Page of Swords (see pp.178–179)

REAL-LIFE READING | Jonathan

Jonathan has just found out that his son Cieron has been accepted to a gifted programme at school. But this means a new environment, without the comfort of familiarity. He looks to the tarot to contemplate how Cieron will be affected by this change. The Celtic Cross was chosen because of its flexibility.

1 A reversed **Emperor** indicates issues with authority; either too little or too much of it.

2 The **Fool** seemingly represents Cieron himself, as an innocent, curious, and open mind that loves to explore.

3 The **Ace of Swords** in the past position seems to accurately depict Cieron's acceptance of a new intellectual opportunity and journey.

4 Temperance Reversed can indicate being pulled in different directions, suggesting that Jonathan may feel worried that as a parent he will have a hard time balancing the needs of his child and other aspects of his life.

5 The **Five of Pentacles** in the future position can indicate feelings of insecurity in an environment among other gifted students, or an unwillingness to seek help during difficult times, and Jonathan may have to pay extra attention to how Cieron is doing to give him the support that he needs.

6 The **Three of Pentacles Reversed** can suggest that there may be an underlying unwillingness to work alongside other students, and perhaps some issues with his peers when he transfers. He may have a hard time making friends or working together with his classmates. Jonathan should be alert to make sure that Cieron is doing well socially.

7 The **Hermit** indicates Jonathan's concerns about switching Cieron over to a new school.

8 Luckily, Cieron's environment is represented by the **Page of Wands**, indicating people who are excited, curious, and inspired, so it is likely that he is surrounded by warm students and faculty that can help him as he gets situated at this new school. So long as Jonathan can encourage Cieron to work closely with others, it seems that Cieron will do well.

9 The **King of Pentacles Reversed** can indicate Jonathan's fears of not doing enough to be a good parent and protector. Jonathan has always been a dedicated father, but worries sometimes – as most good parents do – whether he is doing enough. This can tie into the reversed Emperor that lies at the heart of the spread; what does it mean to be a good father? How does one walk the thin line between giving your child enough space to grow and follow their own pursuits, and guiding them towards success?

10 At the outcome lies the **Page of Swords**, representing an inquisitive, quick-witted and energetic youth with a natural gift for communication. It seems that despite Jonathan's worries, and whatever difficulties that Cieron initially has with his changing circumstances, Cieron will eventually thrive, his new school providing him with a strong environment in which to nurture his mind.

STRENGTH

UPRIGHT
confidence · patience
resilience · inner strength
compassion · diplomacy

REVERSE
self-doubt · insecurity
inadequacy · vulnerability
weakness

UPRIGHT

REVERSE

Interpretation

In order to continue her journey, the Fool must learn to tap into her inner reserves of Strength – the kind that allows one to master and channel their animalistic drives and instincts to succeed despite distress, danger, and struggle. It is not about dominance, but resilience, adaptability, and the confidence that whatever twists and turns life throws one's way, one can handle them calmly.

When Strength is reversed, she can either be lacking in self-assuredness and confidence, or aggressive and volatile. At the core of the Strength card is the symbiotic relationship between our humanity and our animalistic instincts. When the beast is allowed to roam free, her darker urges are not kept in check. She may act brashly, not understanding the impact of her words and actions.

Reflection

How can you call on your inner strength to make the choices that are best for you, even if your fears, colleagues, or family members are discouraging you? This card also signals the discipline and channelling of our more animalistic impulses into constructive action. How can you use these emotions to bring you closer to your ideal outcome?

Are you held back by old fears, apathy, or self-destructive patterns, beliefs, and emotions? What are the things that you believe about yourself? Are they generally positive or negative? It is through showing compassion, towards ourselves and others, that we can develop resilience, empathy, and understanding.

Action

Convert emotion into action Emotional input is a way the unconscious conveys that change needs to be made. This can be internal, like altering how you approach a problem, or external, like leaving your job. If you take action in harmony with those emotions, calm will follow.

Refine your strength Challenge yourself to tap into your inner strength. Whenever you feel a twinge of fear during your day, confront it – tackle the issue head-on instead of shying away from it. Consider this as practice for more important challenges ahead.

Observe your emotions Check in with yourself regularly to notice how you are feeling. Practise this exercise so that you do it instinctively when you are feeling angry or frustrated. This can give you valuable time to think about how best to direct your emotions before acting.

Examine what holds you back Identify self-destructive behaviours and attitudes. Examine narratives that uphold those behaviours. Find the source of these negative beliefs, and question them when they arise. They may rest on weak foundations.

THE HERMIT

UPRIGHT

solitude · withdrawal
retreat · search for wisdom
introspection

REVERSE

isolation · loneliness
feeling lost · disconnected
reclusiveness

UPRIGHT

REVERSE

Interpretation

As the Hermit, the Fool tries to find the wellspring of wisdom that lies within. The Hermit retreats into the dark alone and unafraid. His lantern shines light on the most uncomfortable of places, revealing secrets, hidden motivations, and unresolved fears. He knows that some answers come only when the quiet settles in, when he has time to process the events of his journey so far.

Reversed, the Hermit may be lost in the winding dark paths that lead him to himself. The path of the unconscious can be a dangerous one, for it is filled with our anxieties, projections, and fears. Without an anchor to the outside, he may be led astray. On the other hand, he may be beset with distractions, unable to start his journey, or perhaps unwilling.

Reflection

The Hermit signals a time of introspection and solitude. Are you searching for answers within yourself? Your solitude is an attempt to cultivate an environment of stillness in which you can illuminate the unknown aspects of yourself. Do you feel disconnected from your family and other loved ones? This can be a signal that inner work must be done.

When we are alone too much, having only our echoes to respond to, our reflections of life can become tainted. Has isolation warped how you view relationships, your environment, or the world in general? The reversed Hermit can also signal avoidance. Instead of confronting unresolved anxieties, have you been trying to push them away?

Action

Get in the flow Have you ever felt the intense state of focus that happens when you're so engrossed in an activity that all thoughts fade away? Try to get into this mindful state, whether it's through drawing, running, crocheting, or gardening.

Clear your mind With social media and technology ever present in our lives it's easier than ever to distract ourselves from our own problems. Take a break from tech, and explore the thoughts, ideas, and emotions that come up when there is nothing to drown them out.

Reconnect with the world Whether it's just taking a walk or getting in touch with an old friend, you may find the outside world more welcoming than you remember.

Get another opinion Finding someone to bounce ideas off could be helpful. Seek advice to gain a fresh perspective.

Confront the discomfort Challenge yourself to sit with your discomfort for a little while, and let it sink in. In this way, you can start to poke and prod it, and understand where it comes from and how to banish it.

63

WHEEL OF FORTUNE

UPRIGHT
cycles · fate · fortune
luck · transience
unpredictability

REVERSE
clinging to control · repetition
external circumstances
going round in circles

UPRIGHT

REVERSE

Interpretation

The Wheel of Fortune represents the inevitable; it is the wheel on which the fates spin the thread of everyone's stories. This card is a symbol for the unpredictability and transience of life. However, if we can stand at the centre of the Wheel, we may discover that there is stillness within the chaos. Here we can find serenity and learn to appreciate the beauty of all things that are fleeting.

As the Wheel turns, our fates turn with it. With each rotation there are people who cling to its sides to try and force its direction. This is wasted energy and emotion, and makes the inevitable change that much more painful. Others may search for reasons why the Wheel turns as it does. This can either be a balm to the soul, or create more pain when no answers are found.

Reflection

Do you feel life is out of your control? We are often at the mercy of cycles that we cannot understand or predict. There are larger forces at work, and they sweep us up in their changes. These can be societal, cultural, environmental, economical, or natural; think of a recession, or a natural disaster. What forces do you feel at the mercy of?

Are you finding that as things shift below your feet you are unprepared to deal with them? Are there any changes in your life that you are resisting? Alternatively, if you have felt stuck in a loop, facing the same situations again and again, you may be finally breaking the cycle. Can you now see a path that could lead you back into the normal flow of life?

Action

Accept transience Appreciate the good times when they last, and weather the storms when they come knowing that they will pass. Everything is transitory.

Identify repeating patterns What situations do you find yourself in again and again? It may be a string of bad relationships or conflicts with authority figures. Knowing what themes are present in your life can help you see the same old story before it unfolds.

Find your centre Try to identify what makes you feel grounded regardless of where the Wheel takes you.

Release control When we fail to accept the inevitable, we can harm ourselves. Detach your happiness from external events, and connect with your own efforts. Maybe that project didn't work out as you had hoped, but trying helped you hone your abilities.

Know what you can and can't change The external world – other people, culture, society, the economy – is always shifting. We may not be able to directly influence these things, but we can take responsibility for our own reactions to them. This is where you can find your personal power.

JUSTICE

UPRIGHT
fairness · objectivity · truth
honesty · cause and effect
accountability

REVERSE
unfairness · revenge
injustice · corruption
consequences · retribution

UPRIGHT

REVERSE

Interpretation

Upright, Justice can always be depended upon to uphold the values of fairness, truth, and honesty. Her third eye gives her the omniscient vision to see all actions and intentions and judge them with impartiality and openness. She is representative of the law of cause and effect, which decrees all actions have their subsequent reactions, and at times, consequences.

When Justice is reversed, she can lose her ability to be objective, to see the truth, or to assert consequences. Perhaps she has her own prejudices or biases that are clouding her usual sharp vision. On the other hand, in her desire to make things right, she may have gone too far; she has forgotten that her true values are to correct imbalances in the law of karma, not to punish or injure.

Reflection

The Justice card teaches the importance of accountability. If you have been wronged in a relationship, this card's appearance may bring relief. On the other hand, Justice represents a chance for you to take responsibility for mistakes. What choices do you regret? What does owning up and correcting your mistake look and feel like?

Drawing Justice in reverse can indicate that you are in a situation that has been unfair. Do you feel the need to assign blame to someone at work? Are you filled with a yearning to teach an ex-partner a lesson? Is revenge your main concern? Do you have faith that the universe will create balance? Or do you take justice into your own hands?

Action

Get an outsider's perspective Sometimes we are too close to a situation to be impartial or fair. Find someone honest who can tell you what it looks like from the outside. Make sure you aren't just seeking validation.

Find facts Let truth be your guide. Try to position yourself outside of your subjective viewpoint and see the bigger picture. Notice how this changes your outlook.

Make amends Now is the time to own up to past mistakes. You'll find that most are willing to forgive if you are truly sorry and able to make a change for the better.

Detach from vengeance It is important to strike a balance between defending yourself and maliciousness. Consider what is to be gained from revenge. It is unlikely to solve your problem and the consequences are rarely worth the momentary satisfaction.

Understand your accountability Take a wider view, and consider if you had a part to play in the issue as well. Try to engage in fair discussions with any other injured party.

Trust in karma When things are unfair and there is nothing we can do, remember that everyone will reap what they sow.

THE HANGED MAN

UPRIGHT	**REVERSE**
surrender · sacrifice	release · detachment
inactivity · waiting	being stuck · stalling
acceptance	fear of sacrifice

UPRIGHT

REVERSE

Interpretation

The Hanged Man finds himself upside-down on a cross, apparently unconcerned about his seemingly precarious state. At first he struggled, but quickly learned that this would just deplete his energy, so he let himself relax. With this new perspective, all the cares that he had the day before seem trivial. He also knows that this is the sacrifice he needs to make in order to achieve his goal.

In reverse, the Hanged Man finds himself right-side up again. He may have struggled out of his bonds; perhaps he felt his end goal was not worth the sacrifice of being in this position. Or maybe the bonds that held him have worn out. If he has not struggled, he will have gained a different way of seeing the world, and know that he is one step closer to being where he wants to be.

Reflection

Although you have clear career goals, you realize you must take two steps backwards to correct your course. What are you sacrificing? How does seeing the bigger picture shift your viewpoint of what you are giving up? The Hanged Man also represents the wisdom to know that when the time is right for something to happen, it will.

You may feel as though life is no longer on hold and you can continue along your path. What sacrifices did you have to make to reach this point? Was it worth it? On the other hand, are you frustrated by the lack of progress you've made in pursuit of your goals? Do the next steps depend on other people or external circumstances?

Action

Bide your time Sometimes waiting for the right moment is the best course of action. When the timing is right, events will unfold.

Think of the larger goal Focus on the bigger picture, and the little sacrifices that you make to get there don't seem so bad.

Know what you can't control Achieving certain goals will depend on other people or external circumstances, which are beyond your control. Try to focus instead on what you have power over. Perhaps it's time to look inward rather than outward.

Explore your new perspective Consider how your time in suspension changed the way you view the world. Embrace the new opportunities available to you now – perhaps they have always been there, but you just didn't see them before.

Surrender If you've been struggling to accept the obstacles that are in your way, this card could be a sign that you have to let go sometimes. Accept things as they are.

Give your thinking mind a break Trying to force solutions doesn't always work. When your mind is well-rested, answers may come.

DEATH

UPRIGHT	REVERSE
endings · letting go	decay · resisting change
transformation · rebirth	fear · clinging to the past
moving on · transition	deterioration

UPRIGHT

REVERSE

Interpretation

The kind of change that Death brings with him is not always welcome, but it is necessary. Life is always in motion, and what is here today cannot remain forever, or it grows sickly and stagnant. When Death brings about the end of one chapter, he opens the door to the next. The ending of this stage may be painful, but is ultimately for the greater good.

A world without Death would be one without transition, a world stuck in time. Eventually, a world without death would be a world without life. Death and Life need each other, just as an animal dies and its body decomposes to enrich the soil from which plant life grows. When we cling onto things that no longer serve us we become stuck, we are no longer flowing with the river of life.

Reflection

At the core of the Death card is the concept of transformation. You may have experienced many transitions in your life, but there could be a lingering feeling that this change is different. Are you holding illusions, beliefs, and attitudes that are no longer serving you? Are you in a toxic relationship? What needs to be released in order for you to truly grow?

Death is part of an inevitable cycle, whose purpose is to create new life. How does death help us evolve? When a part of us dies, what remains are aspects of ourselves that are unbreakable and immortal. What parts of your identity are you afraid to lose? What new versions of yourself do you reject and hide so you can feel safe?

Action

Lean in to change Think back to major transformations that you've undergone in your past. Take stock of what was lost, but also what you gained and how you grew. Let these serve as reminders to be excited for change.

Mourn It is natural that when we leave something behind, we feel grief. Be kind to yourself and mourn what is being lost. Appreciate the past selves that helped you get to where you are, but who can no longer take the rest of the journey with you. Thank them, but don't let them hold you back.

Identify decay Determine which beliefs or relationships are not actually working, or now working against you. Consider what could happen if you let them continue holding you back, and what it would take to let them go.

Separate These beliefs or relationships may have become a part of how you see your own identity. For example, maybe you hold on to a toxic relationship with a parent so you can believe you are a good child. Maybe being a good son or daughter is essential to your identity. Illuminate these patterns in your life.

TEMPERANCE

UPRIGHT

moderation · patience
caution · thoughtfulness
peace · alignment

REVERSE

imbalance · excess
extremes · recklessness
caught in the middle

UPRIGHT

REVERSE

Interpretation

At the heart of the Temperance card is the concept of alchemy, of mixing diverse concepts into a greater whole. It is the understanding that multiple viewpoints, perspectives, beliefs, and ideas can be crystallized into something beautiful with thoughtfulness and cooperation. It is through avoiding extremes and taking the path of moderation that excellence can be born.

When reversed, Temperance's attempts to create a harmonious blend of ideas, concepts, feelings, and processes can fall apart. Her powers of alchemy, that would usually unify and transform, yield little fruit. There is refusal to cooperate or compromise. She can also be representative of excesses in one area instead of taking a moderate and balanced approach.

Reflection

You understand that the best outcomes often arise from a blend of different approaches. You may naturally seek the union of many ideas, desires, beliefs and attitudes. Does this individualistic way of dealing with things bring you a feeling of peace? In what areas of your life have you found success through blending and mixing diverse elements?

Do you feel as though you are being pulled in multiple directions? This could be either by people, your environment, or something more internal. Are you in the middle of an argument? Or are your family life and your job competing for your limited time? This card represents a gentle nudge for you to find peace and equilibrium.

Action

Practise gratitude Challenge yourself to appreciate the best of every experience that you have today. Consider what you can learn about each of these experiences that you can incorporate into your life.

Contemplate alchemy This is the art of blending and mixing different elements to create a better whole. Think of an example in your life where the combination of something is better than its parts. Try and appreciate how wonderful things are when they come together versus remaining separate. This can teach you a lot about Temperance.

Identify excess Perhaps your life is out of balance. Maybe you are consistently drinking or partying, or buying too many things that you don't need. Think about what hole these habits are attempting to fill. Consider how these deplete your sense of serenity.

Look for compromises Going too far to one extreme or the other can be damaging right now. Try to reach a middle ground, without overextending yourself in either direction. Blend ideas, viewpoints, methods, and processes in order to find the path that suits everyone well.

THE DEVIL

UPRIGHT

shadow self · repression
addiction · playfulness
temptation · indulgence

REVERSE

independence · freedom
restoring control · release
reclaiming power

UPRIGHT

REVERSE

Interpretation

In order for the Fool to continue her path towards spiritual fulfilment, she must learn to release herself from her attachments and confront her shadow. This is the lesson of the Devil, who embodies the shadow self. He may come with many gifts – external objects or items that she covets, believing that these can either numb the pain of her frailty or be tools for her to gain strength.

When the Devil card is reversed he does not arise menacingly out of the unconscious, but is consciously confronted. He is seen for what he is; a demon that we have created by projecting all our shame, fears, anxieties, and perceived negative qualities onto a symbol. The reversed Devil can also indicate the retreat back into our darkest selves, overcome with shame or guilt.

Reflection

The Devil represents your shadow, the parts of you that your ego despises, fears, and represses in order to feel unblemished. What aspects of yourself are you ashamed of and trying to hide? By rejecting our shadow self, our self-loathing turns outward and projects onto others. What narratives are you addicted to? What is your ego dependent on?

You are in the process of confronting your shadow self, and you may be close to having a breakthrough. Are you breaking the chains of poor habits, maladaptive belief systems, or outworn perspectives? At this juncture your inner demons can make one last push that is stronger than ever. Now is the time to stay rooted in self-awareness.

Action

Separate needs from addictions Perhaps you prioritize one thing to the detriment of everything else, or there are things that you feel you never have enough of. Identify the hole your addictions are attempting to fill. When you feel the craving again, name it; identifying it is the first step to taking conscious action.

Illuminate shadows Don't reject your shadows, but confront and see them for what they are; with this they lose their power. Tenderness to your whole self, imperfections and all, can free you.

Nurture independence Maybe there was something you thought you desperately needed, but later realized that it wasn't integral to your happiness. Think of how liberating it felt to lose that burden, and what you could do now if you had that freedom.

Share your shame Keeping your darkest thoughts secret allows them to fester. When you share what shames you, you may discover that these thoughts aren't as awful or uncommon as you think they are. Bring them to light; explore them with someone you trust.

THE TOWER

UPRIGHT

destruction · collapse
sudden change · crisis
perceived disaster
purification

REVERSE

averting disaster
delaying the inevitable
avoiding truth
embracing transition

UPRIGHT

REVERSE

Interpretation

When the Fool encounters the Tower, she must learn to accept that stagnant structures have to be dismantled, so that what is broken can be purged and create the ground for something stronger. The Tower represents the purifying destruction of foundations and ideologies that are no longer productive. This is likely to be painful and chaotic, but necessary in order to clear the path.

Upright, the dramatic destruction of outworn values and foundations feels forced upon us. Reversed, the Fool may embrace or instigate the much-needed destruction. On the other hand, she may resist, even though there may be an awareness that for every new brick she places on the rickety Tower, the more its foundations begin to tremble, and the more gruesome its eventual fall will be.

Reflection

Our desire to feel safe can conflict with the truth of what is happening outside, so we build thicker walls, and we build upwards, taking us further from that truth. Are you in denial? What outdated beliefs and delusions must crumble now? When we experience a crisis that clears away everything we thought we knew, what does it make room for?

How do you handle crisis? Our reaction to dramatic, foundational changes is at the heart of the Tower reversed. Do you welcome such changes? Are you constantly questioning and illuminating what ideologies or value systems are no longer supporting you? On the other hand, you may be resisting change, fearful of potential turmoil.

Action

Cast a critical eye Re-examine your life and what changes need to be made. It is possible to get ahead of the crisis, and prepare yourself for the transformation.

Trust The dissolution of our core beliefs is not an easy card to deal with, but the Tower indicates that this is something that must happen. Trust that this is for a reason.

Observe destruction Like all dualities, destruction and creation exist in a balance. To deny one would stifle the other. In a moment of anger, maybe you smashed something. Think of how it made you feel afterwards.

Look forward, not back Consider what has room to grow now that illusions and false assumptions have been cleared. Think about what you can welcome into your life.

Embrace past crises Think of a moment when your worst nightmare became a reality, and the ways in which you have grown since then. Consider the new things that came into your life as a result of that crisis.

Understand consequences of inaction Look at how things get worse the longer you choose to ignore a problem. Consider your emotional and mental state.

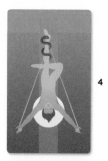

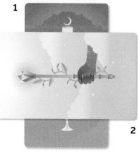

CELTIC CROSS

1 HEART OF THE MATTER
Seven of Cups (see pp.138-139)

2 CHALLENGE
Ace of Wands (see pp.94-95)

3 PAST
Moon (see pp.82-83)

4 CONSCIOUS
Hanged Man (see pp.68-69)

5 FUTURE
Tower (see pp.76-77)

6 UNCONSCIOUS
Three of Pentacles (see pp.192-193)

7 QUERENT
Ace of Cups (see pp.124-125)

8 ENVIRONMENT
Page of Swords (see pp.178-179)

9 HOPES AND FEARS
Knight of Swords (see pp.180-181)

10 OUTCOME
Two of Wands (see pp.96-97)

REAL-LIFE READING | Nyla

Nyla has recently achieved a big milestone in her career, but she is still feeling unfulfilled. Left without any motivation, she is unsure of what she should be doing next, or whether she is on the right path. She wanted a general but comprehensive reading about her career so she used a Celtic Cross Spread.

1 The **Seven of Cups** lies at the heart of the issue; Nyla has many choices, and all of them are promising in their own way. Fantasy and illusion are at work here; she finds herself daydreaming about each possible experience without taking action on any of them.

2 She is having difficulty finding motivation and is lacking energy, represented by the **Ace of Wands**.

3 The **Moon** indicates that she has perhaps been feeling lost in her illusions and her own reflections for a long time.

4 She is well aware that in order to move forward, she must be like the **Hanged Man**, ready to take a step backward and make a sacrifice. This may mean starting over in a new career, or taking a demotion in order to figure out where her heart truly pulls her.

5 The future represented by the **Tower** is a warning. Should she not take action and continue to only daydream, things can shift without her input. She may already be aware that her passion is waning, meaning her work may be suffering. Pretending things are fine may lead to upheaval.

6 The **Three of Pentacles** can indicate an unconscious desire for a position that lets her work more with others. Perhaps her current job has been too isolating, or maybe she doesn't have access to peers.

7 The **Ace of Cups** indicates that in her heart of hearts, Nyla knows that change is needed. She is asking these questions out of care and concern for herself. She recognizes that continuing this position may be damaging to her mental health, and emotionally she is ready for change.

8 The **Page of Swords** can indicate an environment or a person in Nyla's life who is alert, curious, and quick on their feet.

9 The **Knight of Swords** indicates a concern or a desire that the work environment will be taken up a notch; Nyla is a careful person who likes having plenty of time to consider her actions. She may in equal measure find excitement or dread in a fast-paced environment.

10 At the final outcome position, the **Two of Wands** indicates that Nyla will have to stop simply daydreaming about changes, and start making plans for her exit. She must now make decisions on what to do next.

THE STAR

UPRIGHT
hope · faith · healing
regeneration · inspiration
guidance

REVERSE
faithlessness · discouraged
despair · hopelessness
uninspired

UPRIGHT

REVERSE

Interpretation

After the Fool's encounter with the Tower has left her stripped back to her core being, she finds the Star. It is here, even in the rubble of broken systems and cleared delusions, that she recognizes all that she is blessed with. She is filled with a deep faith that she has all that she needs within herself to find fulfilment. The Star knows that the core of her humanity, her spirit, is untouchable.

When the Star is reversed, the Fool's faith in herself and the universe has evaporated. Perhaps the stars are now covered by clouds, and whatever the Fool needed for guidance is being obscured. But in all our hearts, our inner Star can guide us, even through the darkest of nights. The Fool must make the choice to either rise to the occasion and trust in herself, or become lost to the night.

Reflection

You may be in the process of healing from a terrible life challenge. Perhaps you have discovered your own inner strength, resilience, and the immortal light that glows within. How does loss clarify what is eternal in us? Your inner compass has led you through loss, grief, or trauma to be reborn as you are now – more authentic than ever before.

When the light of our inner Star has dimmed, we may experience a loss of hope. What have you lost faith in? Where can you find renewed hope? Reversed, the Star can also indicate being uninspired and bored at work. How can you rediscover your purpose again? What once brought a sense of excitement into your life, and how can you bring it back?

Action

Cultivate optimism There are so many reasons in the day to be cynical and expect the worst. If you find yourself thinking about consequences of taking actions, pause and also think about what is the best that can happen. Consider whether it pays off more to be hopeful or cynical. Think about what you would do if you were not afraid.

Bring light Just as stars guide us all, your inner star can illuminate the lives of your loved ones as well. Think of ways you can radiate light to those around you, and how your life's purpose can bring joy to others.

Find inspiration Surround yourself with art and beauty, or immerse yourself in nature and enjoy some of its healing effects. Your light cannot shine when you are feeling drained, so replenish yourself.

Rediscover purpose Consider what gives you a reason to get up every day. Find something that matters to you, and nourish it.

Just try When we are without hope, we give up before giving ourselves a chance, and failure becomes a self-fulfilling prophecy. Think what you stand to lose if you don't try.

THE MOON

UPRIGHT
imagination · fantasy · habits
instincts · unconscious
losing one's way

REVERSE
fear · confusion
self-deception · anxiety
misunderstandings

UPRIGHT

REVERSE

Interpretation

As the Fool gazes at the moon's reflection on the surface of a lake, the line between the reflection and what is real becomes blurred. Our instincts and feelings affect the way that we perceive the world – what we see around us mirrors our internal landscape. The Moon represents this mirror world of the internal, where our imagination thrives, and our fantasies linger.

When the Moon is in reverse, the sky and the mirrored waters below have merged; we can no longer distinguish what is real, and nothing is what it seems. The Fool sees many fearsome shapes spring up before her – these may be visions of emotions that she has not yet faced, of traumas that were too painful to confront, so she pushed them to the deeper realms of her unconscious.

Reflection

When the Moon is present, our perception is highly affected by our internal narrative. Is reading a situation in your relationship difficult because it activates subconscious triggers? You will need a high awareness of your own character, its lights and its shadows, in order to distinguish between fears that you've created, and those that are real.

The Moon represents all the power of our instincts and emotions; which can lead us towards our best selves, or to an abyssal echo chamber. How do your emotions and instincts affect the way that you perceive the world? What self-deceptions are you holding on to? What negative emotions are you trying to avoid when you cling to these?

Action

Exercise and observe your fantasies Take some time to daydream and consider what types of narratives show up in your imaginings. Perhaps you put yourself in the role of a damsel in distress, or maybe you are a capable problem solver. Examine your desires, your motivations, and the role of others in these daydreams.

Examine your moods Try and name your moods throughout the day. Observe how they colour your interactions and reactions to the world around you. Consider how your internal landscape shapes each day.

Remember this emotion If you're dealing with intense feelings, pause and try to remember when you've felt this before. Think of the similarities between that situation and now. It's likely that this card is indicating unresolved emotions.

Separate behaviour and interpretation It can be easy to misinterpret somone's facial expression and make a judgment about their character or feelings based on this. But think about what they actually did, and what your assumptions were. Consider more possible reasons why people act the way they do.

THE SUN

UPRIGHT	REVERSE
happiness · vitality	negativity · sadness
success · positivity	no enthusiasm
optimism · radiance	overconfidence

UPRIGHT

REVERSE

Interpretation

In Tarot, the Sun is representative of light, warmth, radiance, and life; it gives the Fool energy, strength, positivity, and charisma. The light of the sun shines on her, within her, and through her; she brightens the world with her energy and boundless optimism. With her heart full of love, confidence, and gratitude, it is only natural for the Fool to express her joy, and imbue others with that same joy.

When the Sun is reversed, the clouds cover its life-giving light, and the warmth and the joy that it affords us can be darkened. However, whatever shadow is cast right now is one that will soon fade. But sometimes the Sun can be harsh and relentless, and the warmth of happiness can turn into a burning ardour. The Fool under its light can become too optimistic, impractical, and unrealistic.

Reflection

The energy of this card is vibrant; it is a reminder that after each dark night, there comes a new day. This transformation is at the heart of the Sun card, sacred and wonderful. What does it feel like to be embraced by the sun's warmth? Do you trust that light always returns after darkness? How does this make it easier to accept the night?

Your issues here have a high chance of being resolved, as long as you continue to look forward and remain optimistic. On the other hand, a reversed Sun can indicate that you may be over-confident and unrealistic in your aims. Have your career goals been attainable? What can you adjust to become more grounded in your ambitions?

Action

Define happiness Consider what is it that you are doing when you are happiest. Think about what your happiness looks like and how it changes your outlook towards others.

Bring light Joy is a gift that is meant to be shared so consider how you can let your light shine through to others. Think about ways that you can bring joy, whether it's by doing a favour, or giving a small gift. Explore what it feels like to be able to give.

Play Challenge yourself to do something every day that serves no purpose other than giving you pure enjoyment.

Choose to see possibilities Instead of focusing on what can't be done, try to think about what can. Consider the opportunities around you right now. They may present different methods of reaching your goal, but be just as valid.

Create realistic goals Evaluate your current plans. Do they need to be modified to make them attainable?

Feel illuminated Enjoy being embraced and nourished by the sun and the warmth of its rays. Clouds pass, but the sun, even when not visible, is eternal.

JUDGMENT

UPRIGHT	REVERSE
awakening · evaluation	self-doubt · ignoring calling
reckoning · rebirth · revival	lack of self-awareness
self-awareness	indecisiveness · impracticality

UPRIGHT

REVERSE

Interpretation

When the Fool encounters Judgment, he is hearing the resounding call of his own spirit to look beyond himself. This card symbolizes a rebirth of the soul that comes with new awakenings. This angel on this card is a messenger from one's higher consciousness, beckoning the Fool to live his life with more awareness, so that he can conduct himself with authenticity and enjoy every moment.

Awakening can mean drastic changes may need to be made. When Judgment is reversed, the Fool may be too afraid of what challenges and sacrifices this may entail. He may instead choose to continue with the path that he is on, feeling safe and sheltered in his routines. But the call, when it is not heeded, is not something that goes away. If ignored, it will only get louder.

Reflection

Have you ever experienced a moment of sudden realization that would change your course of actions for good? Those moments fall under the Judgment card. What revelation have you had recently? Which messages can you no longer ignore? These will feel like callings, pulling you from a slumber into full awareness and awakening.

What messages from your higher consciousness have you been ignoring recently? What callings have you failed to answer? You may need to spend some time in self-reflection in order to follow the path that is being asked of you now. This card is a push to let you know that now is the time to wake up and answer the call of your heart.

Action

Follow your purpose Align yourself with your highest purpose, and follow your calling. Now is the time to banish your fears and take the plunge. Strong decisions must be made, and that requires being sure of what your path is. Embrace your rebirth.

Make an honest self-assessment To awaken, we must start by looking at ourselves with honesty. Consider the challenges, successes, and failures you have faced. Make adjustments, but don't linger on what has been lost. Reawaken to your new life with open eyes.

Cultivate self-awareness If you've been on autopilot, schedule daily check-ins with yourself. Try and understand what you've been feeling underneath your detachment. In this stillness that you carve out, notice what emotions, thoughts, and sensations arise. If there is a pattern emerging consider where it might lead.

Don't evade judgment When we realign, it can often coincide with harsh judgments from others. Not everyone will be supportive of our changes. Maybe you avoid rebirth because you fear judgment.

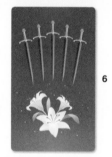

CELTIC CROSS

1 HEART OF THE MATTER
Chariot (see pp.56-57)

2 CHALLENGE
Queen of Swords (see pp.182-183)

3 PAST
Queen of Wands (see pp.120-121)

4 CONSCIOUS
Devil (see pp.74-75)

5 FUTURE
Seven of Penatacles
(see pp.200-201)

6 UNCONSCIOUS
Five of Swords (see pp.164-165)

7 QUERENT
Eight of Pentacles
(see pp.202-203)

8 ENVIRONMENT
King of Wands (see pp.122-123)

9 HOPES AND FEARS
Hermit (see pp.62-63)

10 OUTCOME
Empress (see pp.48-49)

REAL-LIFE READING | Amelie

Amelie experienced some tension between herself and her friends, which precipitated her confronting the problem. This, though, created more hostility. She feels guilty and angry, but wants to put this situation behind her. She is unsure about her conflicting feelings so she opted for the Celtic Cross.

1 The **Chariot** lies at the centre of the spread, indicating the desire for movement, progress, and overcoming guilt.

2 The **Queen of Swords** stands in opposition to this goal; representing the side of Amelie that is separated from her emotions, judging the situation with logic and clarity alone.

3 The **Queen of Wands** signifies there's another side to Amelie – someone who is confident, self-aware, courageous, and passionate. It took courage to speak up. Although Amelie feared it would not be received well, she felt it better to be authentic and honest. There may be a battle raging within; on one side lies cold, hard facts, and on the other passion, self-defence, and perhaps some anger. How can these two aspects of her self be resolved? Can Amelie accept and honour her emotions?

4 The **Devil** in the conscious position represents guilt, which prevents Amelie from seeking freedom beyond an oppressive group. It can also signal feeling trapped and unable to escape oppressive thoughts.

5 The **Seven of Pentacles** indicates that progress is slow; Amelie is on the way toward healing and understanding that conflict was needed, even though there are no obvious changes.

6 Although she may be reluctant to do so, Amelie must leave behind her ego. Her unconscious is already aware that she needs to do this to truly heal, since the **Five of Swords** indicates a conflict with no winners. Both parties need to reconcile in order to move ahead.

7 The **Eight of Pentacles** in the querent position signals devotion and dedication to a craft. The matter that caused the dispute was about Amelie having the freedom to develop and pursue her passions without judgment, limitations, or condescension.

8 The **King of Wands** suggests an environment that needs strong, fearless leadership. Should Amelie want to repair her friendships, she may need to make the first move and reach out.

9 The **Hermit** has a double message; Amelie fears isolation, but she can also use her time away from these friends to find further insights and clarity about her own needs and wants as an individual.

10 At the outcome is the **Empress**, a hopeful sign that there is true happiness beyond this situation. By being grateful for all the things that Amelie has in her life, this conflict will seem small and insignificant. She must create space for herself where she can thrive, grow, and experience new things. She must also learn to nurture, care, and tend to herself as much as others.

THE WORLD

UPRIGHT	**REVERSE**
fulfilment · completion	incompletion · emptiness
mastery · attainment	lack of closure · irresolution
integration	disappointment

UPRIGHT

REVERSE

Interpretation

Finally, the Fool reaches the World and feels complete. This is where the boundaries between self and other, emotion and action, identity and world come together as one. She has found success, in whatever form she has defined for herself, and lives her life authentically. While the Fool revels in this stage, she knows that this cannot be the end, for life is made up of many cycles.

As the Fool is nearing the end of her journey, she is fearful of taking the next step and realizing the goal that she set for herself long ago. Consciously or not, she may be stalling or delaying its resolution. On the other hand, there may be lingering moments of the past that rise up to haunt her – she may need to put some things behind her in order to finally complete her journey.

Reflection

The World upright represents the fulfilment of a long awaited goal. What does it feel like to complete a stage in your life? Alongside joy is there sadness that the journey is over? Life is a never-ending pursuit of new learnings – the completion of one journey heralds the coming of another. What new ground are you preparing?

The World reversed can signal that you are close to completion, but losing focus. What is preventing you from completing this phase of your life? You are being called upon now to tie up loose ends. Alternatively, this card could be signifying a lack of closure. Has a relationship ended, but you are still holding on? What will help you move on?

Action

Appreciate your path Your journey to this moment is a part of who you are. Consider what were the key moments and turning points and how you can use this map of your past to inform and shape your choices ahead.

Celebrate No journey should be without its reward; take some time to enjoy yourself and commemorate this occasion. Savour this moment – you deserve it.

Look ahead Even though one journey is complete, there are always new horizons ahead. Consider what excites you and what makes you curious.

Evaluate wounds Consider what needs to be healed in order to come full circle and move on with your life. Take the first steps.

Tackle loose ends The last steps are always the hardest. It can be tempting to relax just as you are about to complete a large project, so focus is more important now than ever.

Align inner and outer self When our actions and our intentions are not in sync, what we thought would bring us completion can instead feel empty. Consider what is still missing and how you can fulfil your internal objectives.

THE MINOR
ARCANA

The Minor Arcana is a forking path, diverging into four roads,
each reflecting different categories of human experience.
Wands represent inspiration and willpower. Cups embody
emotions and relationships. Swords are concerned with
intellect and logic, while Pentacles signify resources and
the material world. The Minor Arcana comprises our daily
life, our routines, and our immediate circumstances. Like the
Major Arcana, their story is your story. You'll also meet court
cards – characters representing different faces of each suit.
Kings or queens, knights or pages; we can all play their roles.

ACE OF WANDS

UPRIGHT	**REVERSE**
inspiration · ideas	no focus · blocked creativity
creativity · vision	lack of motivation
new projects	creative roadblocks

UPRIGHT

REVERSE

Interpretation

The wands signify creativity and inspiration, and this ace represents the wellspring of creative vision. New ideas have strong potential to become reality, like a spark turning into a blazing flame. Wands channel power and open up possibilities, but these flashes of inspiration are fleeting, and to turn ideas into reality, we must grasp the wand with confidence, excitement, and enthusiasm.

When reversed, creativity and innovation are blocked. There may be either too many ideas with no focus or direction, or a lack of enthusiasm and motivation. Without focus, the wand doesn't know where to direct its energy. Without motivation, the spark of invention dies with no fuel to nurture the flames. There can also be frustrations, impatience, and delays.

Reflection

Passion, motivation, and imagination flood you now. Have you had a sudden flash of inspiration? Or was it a slow and steady build up? What does it feel like in your body? Regardless of whether it is realistic, does an idea keep floating back to you, nudging you to try? What could happen if you put doubts aside and work on realizing your vision?

What smothers your creative spirit? What impediments exist in your professional or personal life right now? Are you easily distracted by new ideas, so you abandon your last one? Do you feel paralysed by all your choices? You may also lack inspiration. Do you feel bored, purposeless, and disconnected? What truly excites you?

Action

Welcome inspiration Open your eyes to possibilities. Look for practical examples of your vision. Search for signs that point you in the right direction. Let inspiration come to you and obstacles may disappear. Maybe a new friend can help you with your project. Perhaps a social media post can spark an idea. Follow the pull of creation.

Channel your energy When you want to do something, run with it. Take one step at a time and see where you go. Do some research, or flesh out an unclear vision.

Don't overthink Now is not the time to analyse, it is the time for action. Sometimes too much thought, doubt, or consideration can lead to paralysis. Harnessing your inspiration sometimes means living in the moment and being aligned with your inner drive.

Search for excitement If you are low on energy, you may do well now to explore new things, and find something that ignites your passion. Go out and take a new class, or pick up a hobby that you've never tried before.

TWO OF WANDS

UPRIGHT
planning · details
making decisions
preparation · exploration

REVERSE
over-analysis
fear of unknown
no direction

UPRIGHT

REVERSE

Interpretation

The Two of Wands moulds new ideas into concrete plans. This card represents the stage of preparation, discovery, and details. The Fool takes the spark of creation and develops long-term plans. He researches and designs his future, then maps a path towards his goal. Here, he leaves his comfort zone, using his courage to create something new.

Well-thought-out plans can become an excessive desire to control one's environment. The Fool must make peace with the fact that some things will always be surprising. On the other hand, he may have no plan at all. He may have enthusiasm but no strategy. Without it, he goes nowhere. Work becomes inefficient; focus must be balanced with spontaneity.

Reflection

Your creative or professional dreams are now coming to fruition. You are taking first steps onto unknown ground; venturing away from the comfort of routine. Do you plan, or are you more spontaneous? Are you excited or nervous? How can you learn what will be required of you? Things are beginning to take shape.

Are you overthinking? When you try to create the safest plan with the highest chance of success, does it stop you from taking action? Does over-analysing come from fear, perfectionism, or low confidence? What do past projects tell you about the way you work towards goals? Knowing your usual style can help illuminate your potential pitfalls.

Action

Step out of your comfort zone Don't be afraid of the unknown. The best kind of learning happens by doing. Work out what could be your first step and don't be frightened to take it.

Design your map Now that you know where you want to go, it can be a great time to plot out all the ways that you can get there. Get concrete; know how your project can affect other areas of your life, explore feasibility. Planning can also help you identify where to find support, and which paths to avoid.

Make peace with unpredictability You can't control everything, so make peace with uncertainty. Your plans may be wonderful, but there will always be something that goes wrong. Understanding the worst-case scenario can actually help decrease anxiety.

Embrace spontaneity Trust that you have the ability to think on your feet, and be realistic about what you can predict. Consider ways to act on your instinct and become more spontaneous.

THREE OF WANDS

UPRIGHT

expansion · progress
momentum · long-term view
stable foundation

REVERSE

obstacles · regret
challenges · frustration
disappointment

UPRIGHT

REVERSE

Interpretation

First steps have been taken to execute plans and pursue dreams. Momentum is great; tasks are being completed, each one taking the Fool closer to his vision. He develops a strong foundation, and confidence grows. His vision expands, too. Empowered, he surveys what lies before him, and realizes that he can do so much more. The future reveals itself to him, full of hard work but also great reward.

Despite best efforts, plans don't always come to fruition. The work may have been done, but for whatever reason, the Fool found obstacles, frustrations, disappointment, and delays. He may regret even having tried. His first steps have proven to be overwhelming. Perhaps he was not ready for all the toil, sacrifices, and challenges that he would face. He may have to revise his original ideas.

Reflection

Your high productivity is helping you make progress towards your creative, personal, or professional goals. What victories have you had recently? It may seem like anything is possible now. Use that excitement; what would you want if you could have anything? What big dreams are you suppressing in the name of being realistic?

It is disappointing to try your best and not get results. All journeys have setbacks; they make the whole story so much more compelling. Past mistakes can show us how we've learned and improved. Are you reconsidering your choices? Have you made errors that can help you refine your approach? What did you learn? How can it make you better?

Action

Celebrate Celebrating your achievements can keep motivation high. When things get tough, it's these moments that can help you maintain optimism.

Expand your vision Now is the time to dream big. Don't let the notion of what is realistic block you from wanting more. Daring to want something can be the first step to making it come true.

Consider your narrative Examine the stories that you tell yourself about success. Often, the way we see ourselves and our abilities ends up dictating our actions.

Change your expectations Give yourself space so you can proceed without being too emotionally caught up in potential disappointment. Try to build extra time and resources into your expectations and see how this changes your emotional responses.

Learn from missteps Inevitable obstacles and missteps don't have to ruin your entire project. Instead of kicking yourself for making mistakes, forgive yourself, and focus on what you've learned. Transform that knowledge into practical action.

FOUR OF WANDS

UPRIGHT
fruition · celebration
returning home · relaxation
satisfaction · community

REVERSE
family discord · transcience
lack of belonging
no security

UPRIGHT

REVERSE

Interpretation

Following the Fool's triumph in the three, she returns home to celebrate. She is welcomed by friends and family, who are proud of her accomplishments. She has been successful; an important milestone was reached. There is comfort and familiarity here, and she feels supported. This card can also depict a wedding, reunion, birthday, or another happy occasion shared with loved ones.

This card may depict a difficult domestic situation. When the Fool returns from her journey, she may find tensions brewing between family members and loved ones. Instead of warmth and comfort at home, there may be coldness and uncertainty. She may not have a sense of home at all. Lacking a place to return to, and people to celebrate with, accomplishments can feel empty.

Reflection

What have you accomplished in your professional, personal, or romantic life lately? Can you now rest, enjoy this sense of stability, and revel in your achievements? This card can also signal a homecoming. Where do you find your sense of home? What makes you feel at ease, safe, and secure? Can a sense of home help you accomplish your goals?

Without a stable home base, we also lack security. A home lets us take risks; when we have somewhere to return if things go wrong we feel free to explore and make mistakes. When we are without a home does everything seem harder? Where or who do you call home? How does it affect your decisions?

Action

Find comfort in home Whether it's relatives or your chosen family, pets, or romantic partners, we all have places and people that make us feel welcome and supported. Bask in the company of those whose love helped you along your road to success.

Take a break Acknowledge the effort it took to get here. It was probably not an easy journey. Take a small break and gather your energy for whatever you need to do next.

Say thank you This may be a good time to show some gratitude for the people who have always made you feel at home.

Make home Home doesn't have to be your family of origin, it can be a family that you choose; friends, pets, partners, anyone who is supportive of your best self. Take the time to work on creating these relationships.

Create cosiness Don't underestimate how much your environment affects how you feel. Coming back from a hard day to somewhere that is cluttered or unwelcoming can negatively impact your state of mind. Try redecorating. Notice how your mood changes when you have somewhere you want to return to.

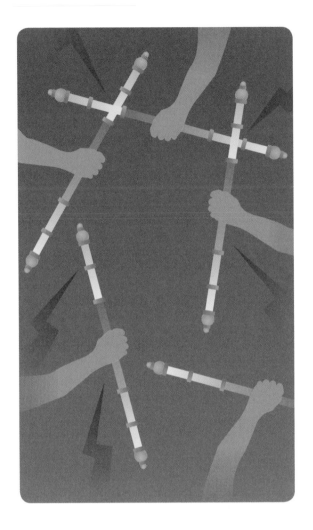

FIVE OF WANDS

UPRIGHT

competition · arguments
disputes · conflict · tension
disagreements

REVERSE

conflict avoidance
jealousy · rising tension
wounded ego · rivalry

UPRIGHT

REVERSE

Interpretation

Tension and conflict are signalled here; many voices are struggling to be heard, and instead of working together, they are fighting for supremacy. There is rivalry, competition, and egotism. The conflict can also be internal, as the Fool sorts out many possible scenarios in her head. To rise above, we must integrate and use the diversity of viewpoints to build something that truly stands the test of time.

The Fool may have trouble dealing with arguments and disputes. This card can signal conflict avoidance, or a sharp escalation of spite and malice between parties. The Fool may shy away from topics that create discord. This card can also indicate the harmful aspects of dealing with rivalries. Jealousy or wounded egos can spark conflicts in an already heated environment.

Reflection

With tension, innocent actions can be construed with malice. Everyone points the finger at each other, ready to fight. How can you avoid being pulled into this? What is the common vision? When others treat us with suspicion we may escalate the situation with anger. Is your ego coming into the picture? How important is it for you to be "right"?

This card is about reassessing how we handle conflict. Often, we must face disputes with the goal of compromise. How do you deal with conflict in your personal or professional life? Do you face it head-on or run away? Are you diplomatic? Do you attempt to make everyone happy at the expense of your own health?

Action

Know your principles Remember your values, and keep them in mind when the going gets tough. Try to stand by them.

Give the benefit of the doubt Try to see the good that others want out of this conflict. Being objective about the intention of others can keep you focused on your own values instead of being frustrated by theirs.

Find common ground Understand others' goals and find places that you can connect. Take criticism constructively, even if it's not intended that way. Consider what feedback can be used for self-improvement.

Notice physical feelings of anger Observe the physical sensations that occur when you are getting angry. This can give you the chance to stop and think before acting.

Remove yourself from the situation If you're caught in the middle of someone else's conflict, this card in reverse can indicate that mediating may come at your emotional expense. Walk away.

Face conflict Sometimes the scariest conversations in our heads are surprisingly simple in real life. Having them now will decrease the chance of resentment later.

SIX OF WANDS

UPRIGHT
victory · triumph
recognition · success
public praise

REVERSE
no rewards · failure
no recognition
low confidence

UPRIGHT

REVERSE

Interpretation

By rising above conflict the Fool has gained the recognition of his peers. He has reached yet another important milestone in his long-term plans, and this has attracted the attention of others. Praise can come in the form of a prestigious award, or a simple pat on the back. He is proud of his achievements, knowing that the admiration is the result of hard work.

Even though the Fool has worked hard, he feels he is not getting the reward that he deserves. A lack of praise has caused him to lose confidence. With no acknowledgment of the effort he has put in, he questions what success really is. Placing too much emphasis on external praise can lead him astray. He must learn to be less dependent on others' opinions, and develop self-trust.

Reflection

You have worked so hard for this day to happen; perseverance and passion has paid off. How will you enjoy your victory? Others may look to you for inspiration and motivation. While this moment is a big win, what is next for you? You've reached a certain level of excellence and the challenges only grow. What do you feel ready to face now?

This card asks us to examine our need for validation. How do you measure success at work, in romance, or elsewhere? Why does getting praise make us feel good? Wanting praise is natural, but not when it becomes a replacement for self-worth. Are you ignoring your internal compass? Have you done something because you want to be "cool"?

Action

Revel in your success Enjoy the praise and recognition you're getting. Share your happiness and your gratitude with those who have helped. You all deserve it!

Get ready for the next step Once the celebrations are over, don't bask too long in the light of your achievements. It's not the time to let your guard down, but instead prepare for what comes next. Keep it up!

Set an example Whether you like it or not, others may be looking to you now as a guide. Find ways to be a positive influence and consider what qualities you want to show.

Display success in your own way Observe how others show success, and differentiate. We are bombarded with messages about what it means to be successful, and these external messages can override our own.

Create your own measurements Consider your own principles and values, and try to build goals and evaluations from these. They can be external, like accomplishing one thing you love every day, or internal – knowing that you did the right thing. With personal standards of success, we simply know that we are worthy just as we are.

SEVEN OF WANDS

UPRIGHT

taking a stand • challenges
defending one's beliefs
persistence

REVERSE

feeling attacked • paranoia
self-victimization
defensiveness

UPRIGHT

REVERSE

Interpretation

The Fool may find herself attacked from all sides and must take a stand to defend herself. Attaining and maintaining success are two different beasts. Others may vie for her position, and she may be defensive and on edge. This card may also be a call to stand with one's principles, even when others are critical. She must maintain higher ground, regardless of whether others are playing dirty.

When anticipation of stress and danger becomes constant, we get the reversed Seven of Wands. The Fool may feel exhausted, ready to give up. She may feel overwhelmed from being constantly vigilant and defensive. Her perpetual state of alertness causes more stress than is needed. When she expects trouble, she seems to attract more of it.

Reflection

Our values form a core part of our identity; when they are attacked, it can feel deeply personal. When was the last time you voiced a deeply held principle, only to be criticized for it? How did you react? Does defending your actions, beliefs, and values fire you up or wear you out? Did you successfully hold your ground, and was it worth it?

Have you ever felt like the world was against you? Do you feel attacked by well-meaning family members or colleagues who judge your choices? Have you felt others were out to get you only to discover a misunderstanding? Does feeling victimized stem from past wounds? How can you clear up the communication?

Action

Take the long view This is going to be an endurance test, so conserve your energy and do what you need to do in order to protect yourself, but do it wisely.

Stand for something When you act with conviction and fight for a cause greater than yourself it can be the fuel you need to keep going.

Be prepared and alert You stand a better chance of making it through the gauntlet if you know what you're signing up for. Face your challenges with knowledge of what to expect and success will be more likely.

List your burdens Knowing what or who you feel attacked by and seeing that the list is finite can help you get a better grasp of reality. It can also guide you towards dealing with issues one at a time.

Remain objective When you're defensive or negative, it's hard to view things realistically. The way we see the world is a reflection of our inner world, and now both may be filled with conflict and stress. Examine what your inner world reflects right now and how this is impacting on the situation. Try to step away and examine the issues more objectively.

EIGHT OF WANDS

UPRIGHT

movement · energy
swiftness · progress
sudden change

REVERSE

chaos · no direction
obstacles · delays
resisting momentum

UPRIGHT

REVERSE

Interpretation

Now is a period of swift progress and unfettered movement. Much energy is suggested by this card, propelling the Fool towards her goals. It may be a busy and productive time, fuelled by newfound vigour. If she flows with that energy and channels it towards a single focus, she can accomplish much. This is a time for the Fool to utilize this vitality and move without delay.

Intense, frantic energy can leave the Fool without focus or a clear vision. She may make mistakes as she rushes, or waste this energy on actions with no purpose. There may be obstacles, blockages, and frustration. This card can also signify resisting momentum; while life's events may be quickly pushing the Fool in one direction, she may consciously or unconsciously fight this.

Reflection

It is a period of frantic progress in your professional, romantic, or personal life; is all your effort paying off? What excitement has entered your life lately? Quick decisions are required. How do you deal with frantic energy? Are you organized or reactive? To make use of this time, can you be purposeful and focused? Be open to opportunities.

Life may be chaotic now, without direction or intention. Are you feeling scatterbrained? Do you waste your time on insignificant and purposeless tasks? Does life moving at a faster pace scare or excite you? If you dislike being forced to make swift decisions, this can be a difficult time. Can you move with the flow of energy instead of against it?

Action

Go with the flow Follow the course of events and harness the momentum. Things may happen quickly, and it may be hard to stop things in their tracks with the amount of energy behind them. Say yes to things that come your way – don't fight this flow.

Direct the course All the wands are moving in parallel, not getting in each other's way. Together, they are a force to be reckoned with. Where do you want them to land? With enough focus you may be able to influence their movement.

Align your goals If priorities are scattered, try to use this energy to work on the tasks that lead you towards your intended direction, and put the others aside.

Trust your instincts They won't fail you. It may be tempting to over-analyse, but during times that call for quick decisions, your unconscious may already know what the right answer is. If something feels exciting, follow that feeling. If something feels off, acknowledge it and act accordingly. Let your first impressions guide you.

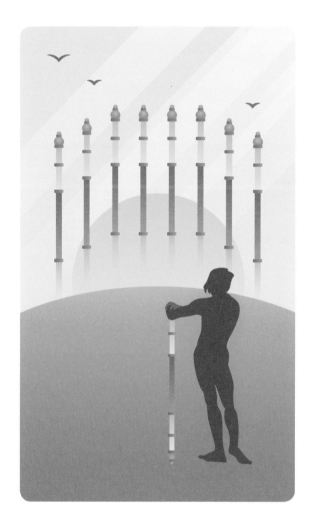

NINE OF WANDS

UPRIGHT

perseverance · determination
adversity · exhaustion
last stand

REVERSE

giving up · stubbornness
rigidity · inflexible
retreat · burnout

UPRIGHT

REVERSE

Interpretation

Trials and tribulations have defined the wands, and the Fool is bruised and battered from strain. Exhausted and humbled, he stands with great determination. Pure willpower and perhaps stubbornness have got him this far. This card is about establishing and protecting boundaries. A line has been drawn, and the Fool has defended himself to both great success, and great cost.

Resolve is lost; many challenges and obstacles stand in the way, and the Fool buckles under stress. He is ready to give up. Alternatively, this card signals that too many boundaries have been built, suspicion and fear leading to defensiveness. The long and arduous struggle has taught him that to survive he must create defences, but these can become a self-made prison.

Reflection

Think about an adversity you successfully overcame in your personal, romantic, or work life. How do you feel looking back on it? Let your resilience be motivation for what you're dealing with now. Did you have more strength than you thought? Look at your battle scars, too. What price did you pay for success? How did it shape how you deal with challenges?

Are you ready to give up? In difficult moments, we can choose to dig in, or let go. It's a fine balance. If you've felt like this before but pushed ahead, what were the results? If you didn't, do you wish you had kept trying? Consider the regrets you could have now. What would you regret more – taking a stand and failing, or walking away without knowing?

Action

Take pride in effort When we approach something new, we are likely to make mistakes. Developing resilience is learning to not beat yourself up for these mistakes. Failure doesn't need to feel humiliating. Detach emotionally from the result of your efforts; take pride in the effort itself.

Protect boundaries Examine the boundaries that are important for you to maintain, and consider what to do if others violate them. Know ahead of time what you are willing to do in order to maintain your wellbeing.

Reassess boundaries Consider whether they protect you or isolate you. Boundaries are healthy, but can become limiting. Think about the benefits of letting others in and weigh them against the risks.

Re-establish reasons Reconnect with the reasons for this fight, and let that invigorate you to march forward.

Recognize wounds Life's lessons can be difficult; everyone develops scars. Be sure your defensiveness isn't the result of bitterness from dealing with challenges.

TEN OF WANDS

UPRIGHT	**REVERSE**
responsibility · strain	burnout · collapse
overstretched · obligation	taking sole responsibility
heaviness	burdens

UPRIGHT

REVERSE

Interpretation

The Fool has overcome many struggles, each one more difficult than the last. But now he realizes that his efforts are still not enough. He is burdened with the heavy responsibility of maintaining his success. He has many duties and people who depend on him. Success comes with a stark awareness that challenges keep coming, and all things worth having require blood, sweat, and tears.

Heavy burdens are marked here, ones that the Fool may be stubbornly resistant to sharing, even as he buckles under their weight. He must either ask for help or share the emotional weight of a secret that he has carried alone. But instead of reaching out, he may push others away. If he does not learn to share his burden, all that he has achieved up until this point may be at risk.

Reflection

Accomplishment always comes with more responsibility; even maintaining the status quo can feel unbearable. Is there always more work to do? What requires resources, energy, and time you don't have? No matter how much effort you put into something, it may not feel enough. What are the limits of working alone?

What burdens do you carry that are not really yours? What emotional consequences are there to carrying the weight for others? What does this express to those you want to help? What do others lose out on when they don't carry their own weight? How does it fail to help them grow? How does it affect your own wellbeing?

Action

Ask for assistance Your burden doesn't have to be yours alone. Others who care for you may be ready to help.

Know your talents Understand what you are good at, and where you lack experience or interest. By valuing your own time, you'll know what is worth delegating to others. Even if it just means paying extra for grocery delivery or a cleaning service perhaps it's worth it if it means feeling less overstretched.

Prioritize tasks Take things one step at a time. Work through your tasks by urgency and importance.

Give space Refrain from jumping into other people's problems and taking control. Sometimes, the best thing one can do for another is step back and let them make mistakes, and do things in their own way. It may be difficult to watch loved ones hurt, but trust that they are capable.

Create limits Knowing when to stop for the day is a kindness that you can show yourself. Set a limit to the time you work, the people you're helping, or the amount of simultaneous projects you're working on. Make sure you don't wear yourself out.

PAGE OF WANDS

UPRIGHT

enthusiastic · energetic
adventurer · possibilities
explorer

REVERSE

unreliable · wasted energy
indecisive · delays
disorganized

UPRIGHT

REVERSE

Interpretation

The Page of Wands is full of curiosity and excitement for life. Everything has potential – each person, each thing, each opportunity is the chance to explore something new, to learn, and to find adventure. She doesn't have a plan, or an idea of where she is going, but the Great Unknown calls to her, and she's itching to get out there. She must follow the calling that pulls her towards new heights.

When the Page of Wands is reversed, her excitement and curiosity for new things can make her disorganized and ineffective. She may work to make her vision real but finds unforeseen complications, and the usual fire that burns bright within her dims. This reversed Page may feel the stirrings of new discoveries within her, but is unable or unsure of how to bring them to life.

Reflection

Can you let this spark of excitement within you ignite? What new experiences and adventures are awaiting you in romance, your personal life, or your career? This can be a good time to take risks. What do we block ourselves off from when we are cautious and safe? New worlds are out there – can you be spontaneous and daring?

Do you feel disheartened? What prevents you from expressing your usual excitement and fervour? Has your routine become dull? New challenges can clear away apathy. Do you want to set out on a new journey, but can't settle on something concrete? It is beautiful to be passionate about everything, but are you spreading yourself too thinly?

Action

Experiment This is the time to try out new ideas. Each can hold the potential for a great new passion. Satiate your curiosity and allow yourself to explore.

Say "yes" When opportunities or chances come your way, take them! Every person you meet is an opportunity to make a new friend and every visit to a new place has the potential to become an adventure. Opening your heart to new experiences can take you to places you never thought you'd see.

Find something to look forward to Whether it's a small treat or a goal that you slowly work towards, everyone needs a reason to get up in the morning. Discover yours.

Make plans If you want to make a change, put together a strategy. As you think through details, it becomes easier to make things happen.

Be spontaneous Get out of your routine and do something unexpected. Even if it's as small as taking a new route to work, or chatting to a stranger on your commute, get out of your comfort zone.

KNIGHT OF WANDS

UPRIGHT	**REVERSE**
brave • hasty • eager	impulsive • cocky
temperamental • ambitious	volatile • violent
capricious • unpredictable	forceful • superficial

UPRIGHT

REVERSE

Interpretation

This Knight channels his excitement and motivation into creative action. Fuelled by fire, he launches himself into projects with gusto. Some may call him reckless; others call him courageous. He is spontaneous, impatient, and prefers action over asking questions. This can lead him into trouble, but he handles it with style. He charges into situations with only his brave spirit and his confidence.

This Knight is a raging fire, and reversed he can become wild and frenzied. He is already temperamental and impatient in nature, so when he runs uncontrolled he can be unpredictable and angry, making hasty decisions, creating destruction in the process, and ignoring consequences. He must make sure that he doesn't burn himself out and accidentally smother his own flames.

Reflection

This is a day for bold actions in romance, your personal life, or at work. Don't let overthinking slow you down. Can you pick a goal and go for it? How spontaneous are you? Do you often get bogged down by details? How do you deal with an unpredictable environment? Your greatest allies will be your courage and confidence.

Have you ever had a fleeting obsession? Were you briefly engrossed in either a person, a hobby, or a subject before quickly losing interest? Passions arise and burn out, but can you now make a choice that lasts? What problems can't be solved by charging through them? What requires a degree of flexibility now?

Action

Trust you can handle new situations Part of heading down an unknown path courageously is knowing you can deal with situations as they arise. Work less on planning, and more on your courage.

Keep your goal in sight Don't lose sight of what you're here for. Keep your vision in mind, and march towards it with determination.

Charge forward Now is the time for action. You may be going in to a situation a little blind, but sometimes in order to accomplish your desires, you have to act now and ask questions later.

Make commitments Keep yourself accountable. If you're someone who starts a lot of projects without finishing them, make sure you stick with them. Find an accountability partner or break things down into smaller goals. Do anything that keeps your passion alive.

Be flexible Sometimes being like water can bring more success than acting like a stone. Water flows around obstacles, a stone will eventually break under continued pressure. You may find more success if you are more adaptable and less stubborn.

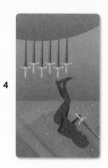

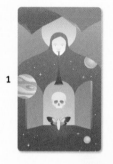

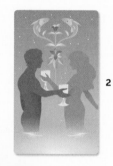

RELATIONSHIP DYNAMICS

1 SELF
Judgment (see pp.86-87)

2 OTHER
Two of Cups (see pp.128-129)

3 RELATIONSHIP
Page of Wands (see pp.114-115)

4 EXPECTATIONS
Seven of Swords Reversed
(see pp.170-171)

5 STRENGTHS
Four of Cups
(see pp.132-133)

6 WEAKNESSES
Lovers (see pp.54-55)

REAL-LIFE READING | Chloë

Chloë has recently ended her long-term relationship, and has met someone new. She is drawn to him, but unsure of his intentions and feelings. She is looking to the tarot to help her understand if she should pursue this relationship. To explore this, she is using the Relationship Dynamics spread.

1 A drastic change, perhaps an awakening of some sort, is indicated by the **Judgment** card. After many years with a previous partner, Chloë came to the striking realization that they just weren't compatible. This card refers to the choice to end that past relationship in order to pursue a romantic partnership that is truly fulfilling.

2 There is the potential for a new partner, represented by the **Two of Cups**. This may not just be a romantic match, but also an equal and balanced partner. There are similar visions, values, and goals for life.

3 The dynamic between them is symbolized by the **Page of Wands**; this connection brings new excitement and a lust for adventure and life that has been missing for a long time.

4 In the expectations we find some trouble. The reversed **Seven of Swords** indicates that there is a degree of deceit or self-deception at work. Chloë second guesses her feelings, wondering whether they are due to the initial excitement and attraction that comes with any new lover, or if they are truly grounded in reality. If she has been hurt in the past, this card can also indicate the fear of being lied to, or the fear of betrayal. She must learn to let go of past suffering in order to see this potential relationship for what it is, instead of what she fears.

5 The **Four of Cups** in the strengths position can indicate that a sense of detachment will be helpful. It may be better for Chloë to take the time to sort out her emotions, her past, her desires, and her fears. This card points to the idea that contemplation on these will be truly helpful in getting some clarity.

6 A rather tricky card to get in the weaknesses position, especially for a love reading, is the **Lovers**. This card would normally be a great card to draw, but here it can indicate trouble. Lovers represents choices and commitment, alongside emotional balance and harmony. Chloë is someone with intense emotions, and tends to get into relationships quickly. Without some deeper contemplation of her desires, fears, and expectations, this can be an issue. It may be more helpful to revisit this question after she does the necessary internal work.

QUEEN OF WANDS

UPRIGHT
cheerful • extroverted • warm
fun • disorganized
sensual • passionate

REVERSE
jealous • fickle
spiteful • vicious • bully
troublemaker

UPRIGHT

REVERSE

Interpretation

The Queen of Wands burns with bright confidence, optimism, and determination. She doesn't expect to be liked by everyone, but regardless is a charming social butterfly. Her determination and exuberance help her to achieve goals. Fully aware of the influence that she has, she loves being the centre of attention. She has the power to spark a great fire in others.

Reversed, this Queen can lose her exuberant charm and self-assuredness. Knowing she cannot please everyone doesn't usually deter her from being her authentic self, but now she may suffer a crisis of confidence. She may stay at home, hiding, or change herself to fit different ideals. Alternatively, her fiery nature may run uncontrolled; she can be spiteful and malicious.

Reflection

This card challenges us to live every day to its fullest and harness our personal power. Every soul has an inner light. How do you let yours shine? Can you express who you are without fear, guilt, or shame? The more authentically we embody our true selves, the more we also appreciate the beauty of others. What is your unique beauty?

What has extinguished your inner fire? What makes you lose your belief in yourself? When we lack self-worth, we may take it out on others. Jealousy and a raging temper are associated with this reversed Queen. She can stir up trouble just out of spite. How do you lash out? What happens after the anger subsides? Is it difficult picking up the pieces?

Action

Celebrate your quirks Enjoy what makes you, you. Appreciate your strengths and flaws; they make you beautiful and unique. Don't censor yourself, behave authentically.

Connect Charisma is strong with this card, so go out and enjoy yourself and the company of others. Your light and warmth will brighten the world. Share your fire!

Explore your shadow self This Queen is a bright but volatile character; celebrating her light as well as her shadow self. Explore the side of you that you hide from others, and what can happen when you are fully seen.

Nurture your inner child If there's been a storm of drama around you recently, analyse whether you play into harmful dynamics. When we are missing self-worth, we unintentionally create issues with others. Explore your inner child's wounds and the ways you could heal these entrenched hurts.

Recognize outbursts We can hurt others when we are feeling pain ourselves. Consider your words and their effect, and think about how you can salvage those relationships. More conscious understanding of your moods can help you recognize triggers.

KING OF WANDS

UPRIGHT
inspirational · honourable
hot tempered · decisive
visionary leader

REVERSE
powerless · ineffective
dictator · domineering
weak · arrogant

UPRIGHT	REVERSE

Interpretation

This King transforms the fiery energy of the wands into creative action and inspiration. He is a natural born leader that can mobilize others. He has a quality that makes people believe in his ideas and encourages them to lend their support. He is inspiring, capable, and big-picture oriented. His ideas are grand and ambitious, and he pursues them with determination and drive.

Even if he has the ideas and creative ability, this reversed King is uncomfortable with the idea of leadership. Perhaps he lacks communication skills. He may feel as though he is better off working alone, or that he doesn't need others to execute his goals. Alternatively, he can be someone who is ruthless and aggressive to the detriment of those around him.

Reflection

What kind of leader are you? You may now be more charismatic, persuasive, and inspirational than usual. Do you wilt at the idea of being in charge or do you take on the role proudly? How does a good leader direct others towards their vision? Do they lead by example, with emotion, or with a strong plan? How can you best direct those around you?

Failure in leadership is marked by this card. If you have the responsibility to lead are you doing it well? Bad leaders can be tyrannical and demanding, driven more by ego than a vision. Or are you in a position with a terrible manager? Do their insecurities manifest in their leadership style? You're likely not alone in feeling worn; revolution is in the air.

Action

Envisage the best possible circumstance Give people something to believe in. This starts with finding your own passions and dreams, which when communicated can compel others.

Take charge Sometimes leadership means believing in our own vision enough to take the first steps. When others see this fearlessness and determination, they naturally follow.

Encourage and motivate Encourage others to be the best versions of themselves so they can take your vision and run with it.

Take a step back Whether it's due to your disinterest or lack of experience, it may be better for someone else to take the reins and lead right now. Observe and see what you have yet to learn.

Lift up others To lead is also to serve. Part of a leader's responsibility is helping others achieve their highest potential. Encourage someone else's growth today.

Get involved True leaders lead with action. Get your hands dirty – nothing should be too lowly. Stay in touch with the people you lead, connect with their concerns.

ACE OF CUPS

UPRIGHT
friendship · compassion
emotional fulfilment
release

REVERSE
drained · repressed
empty · isolated
disconnected

UPRIGHT

REVERSE

Interpretation

This card presents a moment of emotional awakening; new, denied, or repressed feelings are overflowing. This fresh emotional energy can take the form of a new friendship, romantic relationship, or emotional release. The self is the origin of love; by being filled with love, it flows to others. Guards can be let down and the Fool can open herself to joy. Grasp the cup and drink deeply.

Reversed, the gift offered by the Ace of Cups goes wasted, poured out from the chalice, which is now empty. Disconnected from universal love, the Fool is unable to experience the true depth of her emotions. She may be drained, fearing that if she allows herself to feel, the rest of her unaddressed emotions will pour out with destructive intensity.

Reflection

Are we more successful when we act from a place of love? Love starts from the inside, through learning to love and care for oneself with forgiveness, empathy, and patience. Do you love yourself, faults and all? When we are too hard on ourselves, we often judge others harshly, too. How can you become more open to love?

What prevents you from accepting and giving love? How do you react to care and affection? The cup has drained; where there was plenty, there is only emptiness. Do you feel hollow and depleted in your romantic or personal life? How can you replenish yourself, so you may again feel connected and close to the world?

Action

Forgive your flaws Consider the aspects of yourself that you are especially critical of and try to be more accepting of those qualities. Address these parts of yourself with kindness.

Open your heart Allow yourself to be open to new emotions. Try to label your feelings as they arise. Recognizing feelings comes with time and practice.

Follow your heart Challenge yourself to understand where your feelings are coming from, and what actions your emotional self wants to take. Allow yourself to be led by these feelings and see where it takes you.

Recharge Discover what invigorates you. Nourish yourself with whatever you need to feel restored. Focus on your own self-care before you shift your focus outwards again.

Say "thank you" If you find yourself feeling guilty or ashamed when receiving help or compliments, brushing off positive things that people say about you, or apologizing for being a nuisance when others want to lend a hand, try something different. Perhaps what you really mean is "thank you", instead of "sorry". Try expressing gratitude and notice the shift in how you feel.

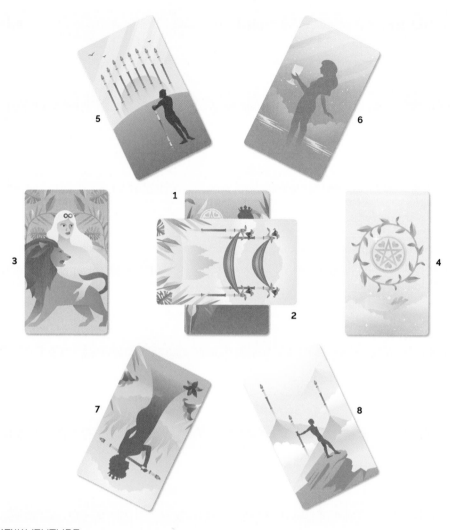

NEW VENTURE

1 MOTIVATION
Queen of Pentacles
(see pp.214-215)

2 CHALLENGES
Four of Wands Reversed
(see pp.100-101)

3 EMOTIONAL GOAL
Strength (see pp.60-61)

4 PRACTICAL GOAL
Ace of Pentacles (see pp.188-189)

5 WHAT YOU OFFER
Nine of Wands (see pp.110-111)

6 WHAT MAKES YOU SPECIAL
Page of Cups (see pp.148-149)

7 ROUTINE
Queen of Wands Reversed
(see pp.120-121)

8 POTENTIAL
Three of Wands (see pp.98-99)

REAL-LIFE READING | Vihan

Vihan has a side project that is finally getting traction, and he is overjoyed. As it grows, however, it needs more time and resources from him. He is currently considering whether it is viable to quit his full-time job and put all of his effort into building this project into a business. He is using the New Venture spread.

1 The motivation for creating this new business is represented by the **Queen of Pentacles**. Clearly, this project is about bettering his financial situation. The desire here is to live well, feel capable and practical, as well as be able to nourish loved ones with an improved material situation.

2 A big part of the decision lies in whether Vihan will be able to support his family. The challenges represented by the **Four of Wands Reversed** signal this; Vihan has a young child, as well as a wife who also works. Even though he feels strongly about this creative project, there are difficulties getting his wife's support. Parental responsibilities may be especially weighing. There is the need to earn trust, and balance ambition with practical realities.

3 Vihan hopes that this new venture can help him develop his confidence and resilience, represented by **Strength**. His current full-time position is not especially demanding; a part of the reason he wants to work on this new venture is likely because he does not feel challenged in his present employment. If it is not practical to leave work right now, he may have to contemplate how to address this. What can Vihan do to scratch his creative itch at his current position? Can he make less drastic changes that aren't as risky as walking away?

4 His practical goal is the **Ace of Pentacles**, which seems to indicate that he just wants the opportunity to simply try. Even though he wishes for ultimate success, he is not expecting it immediately. The possibility for success is something that is tantalizing enough for him.

5 Vihan is someone who won't quit, no matter what, represented by the **Nine of Wands**. This sense of determination and drive is something that he brings to his new venture. Future customers and clients will be impressed with his dedication.

6 His playfulness and imagination, represented by the **Page of Cups**, ensures that his work stands out from that of his competitors. Vihan should use both of these qualities to his advantage.

7 He will have to beware of lapses in confidence, represented by the **Queen of Wands Reversed**. Part of why he pushes himself so hard may be because he doesn't have the self-assured confidence of the upright queen. We already learnt that an emotional goal of his is to develop confidence as well.

8 At the final outlook for this new venture, we find the **Three of Wands**, a card that suggests a growing momentum for creative projects. For the best chance of success, he must keep this momentum up.

TWO OF CUPS

UPRIGHT

attraction · partnership
emotional bond
romantic connection

REVERSE

inequality · imbalance
incompatibility · lack of trust
disharmony

UPRIGHT

REVERSE

Interpretation

This card represents the emotional bond shared between two people. There is the potential for an enduring relationship, with shared compassion, attraction, and the desire to support each other's goals. They can work towards a similar vision for the future together. This card is not limited to romantic relationships, but can also represent platonic friendships and work-based partnerships.

In reverse, this card signals a relationship in disarray. There may be miscommunication, lack of fulfilment, or tension and coldness. Perhaps one person is guarded, suspicious, or distant. Trust is getting difficult to maintain. The Fool must have a foundation of self-love, for it precedes love for others. Wounded egos must be put aside, and she must speak from a place of understanding and care.

Reflection

What does an equal partnership mean to you? What aspects of life do you consider are important to keep in balance with another person? Retaining this equanimity requires us to constantly adjust as the pace of life changes. How can you communicate so that you can adapt and ensure that the attraction between you remains strong?

Are you operating from a place of pure intent and compassion? When trust erodes, work must be done by both parties in order to rebuild it. How did alignment and balance disappear? What must be restored? Can you communicate old resentments in order to let them go? Bitterness builds when we place too much importance on wounded egos.

Action

Show you care Send a thoughtful message or a little gift. Small gestures of affection are often meaningful to others and help nurture a relationship. Love can sometimes be taken for granted, and everyone needs a reminder that they are seen, and cherished.

Re-align As time marches forward, we change, but through commitment you can maintain your relationship. Consider what needs a little adjustment. Speaking with your partner before imbalances become extreme can help avoid fights and resentments later on. Check in with one another.

Air past hurts Frustrations can accumulate when you ignore seemingly insignificant tensions. When we don't communicate what bothers us, it builds up, becomes toxic, and can turn into distrust and anger. Let the issues come to the light; we clear the darkness when we bring it to the surface.

Understand insecurities Self-knowledge is so important – try to take an objective view of your insecurities and explore where they originate from. Communication with your partner can help them to be more sensitive and aware of what triggers these feelings.

THREE OF CUPS

UPRIGHT
friendship · social circle
party · collaboration
celebration

REVERSE
isolation · gossip
cattiness · independence
competitiveness

UPRIGHT

REVERSE

Interpretation

Friendship and social gatherings are at the heart of this card. When the Fool expands her love towards more people, she finds friendship, camaraderie, mutual support, and compassion. This card can also indicate social events, parties, weddings, birthdays, and holidays; anything that brings people together. When it comes to creative projects, this card also relates to collaborations.

When this card is reversed, three is a crowd. There can be a desire to be alone and the Fool may feel stifled in social situations. Groups stymie her creative independence when others are unwilling to embrace a different approach or belief system. She may have to sacrifice some of her freedom for the sake of her friendships. This card can also signal feeling excluded.

Reflection

How important are friendships to you? What makes a good friend? What brings you together? Social circles can shape our identities; through others, we find mirrors for ourselves. Friends point out blind spots and help us see things about ourselves that we take for granted. Has a friend helped you understand yourself better?

Do your friendships feel unfulfilling? What is missing? Friendship is a powerful aspect of our lives that we can sometimes take for granted. As we grow into adulthood, friends take a back seat to romantic partners, family, and careers. How much effort do you put into friendships? Those with strong foundations survive. Have yours lasted?

Action

Learn from friends Think back to a lesson that a friend taught you about yourself, and consider how your perspective changed. It is through friendship that we can grow emotionally. Be open to friends' teachings; they can be strong inspirations for you now.

Widen your social circle Every new person you meet can be a source of inspiration, support, and compassion.

Enjoy Happy times are here – sit back and enjoy being around others. Comfort can be found within your social circle.

Reconnect Without putting in the effort, all things can wither. Think of friendships that were once a strong source of support, and what stands in the way of you reconnecting with them. Even if it's initially awkward, getting in touch with old friends can provide great rewards.

Identify negativity Friendships should be helping you grow, not restraining you. Examine whether you have friendships that are fuelled by negativity, and consider how they affect you. Notice the habits you have learned – it may be wise to create distance.

FOUR OF CUPS

UPRIGHT
apathy · detachment
contemplation · indifference
lack of interest

REVERSE
enthusiasm · awareness
new experiences
motivation

UPRIGHT

REVERSE

Interpretation

New opportunities are around every corner, but the Fool is too unmotivated or indifferent to see them. They instead feel like heavy burdens. Environment and routines can feel dull, uninspiring, and disconnected. The Fool may instead choose to contemplate, coming out of these moments wiser, and with a deeper appreciation for the opportunities that are granted to him.

A wake-up call is in order here. The Fool may have been in a period of contemplation and withdrawal, feeling disconnected from the world; whether things went well or badly were of no concern. This card reversed signals a new awareness, with sudden consciousness of the transient beauty of life. It is imperfect and fleeting, but the choice to see the beauty is what gives life its purpose.

Reflection

When we stop focusing on the present moment, we lose sight of the gifts life offers us. What prevents you from enjoying the present? Are you stuck in the past, or always worrying about the future? These things can distract us from the beauty and the wonder that is unfolding in front of our eyes. What hinders your ability to receive joy?

What sights and sounds of the world feel new to you? What has passed you by when you were in contemplation? What do you need to reconnect with? It is a good time to consider the lessons you learned in your time away from the material world. What changes do you need to make now in order to live without apathy?

Action

Identify expectations Examine how your anticipation affects your disillusionment. When we have high hopes that are dashed by reality, we can be severely disappointed. Take a closer look at whether your forecasts were really reasonable. You may have more to be thankful for than you initially thought.

Search for motivation Identify what has become stale, and what could enliven your situation. Perhaps you need a new challenge, or a change of environment. Discover what excites you.

Review lessons Consider the lessons you learned during your introspection, and how they have changed you.

Apply lessons With inner change, action must follow. You need to re-align with your new self. Examine what you need to do, let go of, or embrace in order to step into this new version of yourself.

Reconnect with your self When we emerge renewed from our inner retreat, not all aspects of our old selves will have survived. Identify the parts of yourself that remain, and pursue them with renewed vigour.

FIVE OF CUPS

UPRIGHT
loss · pessimism
despair · disappointment
grief · regret

REVERSE
forgiveness · moving on
resilience · recovery
looking forward

Five of Cups

UPRIGHT

REVERSE

Interpretation

When expectations are dashed, there can be disappointment and loss. The Fool may be stuck looking backwards, ruminating on her pain and regrets. Three cups have spilled, but two remain upright. This means that the situation, though painful, can be salvaged. The loss is not as severe as the Fool makes it out to be; there is still so much to enjoy. She must leave mistakes behind and look ahead.

The Fool shows a significant recovery from the loss and regret that prevented her from fully experiencing life. Mistakes are seen from a larger perspective; they do not define her, but still have value by shaping her life going forward. Through the grief and the sadness she has been endowed with resilience, and is now more aware of her own strength. She is ready to move towards a brighter future.

Reflection

Are you lost in feelings of despair and sadness? When you experience disappointment it is a time to grieve, but not all is lost. How will you preserve and protect what can be salvaged? How can you reframe your perspective, and make peace with the past? Can you find the comfort and inspiration you need to move forward?

You may have been dealt hardships, but are you seeing them as chances to grow? Are you ready to re-join life? Are life's events inherently good or bad? Or do they only have the meaning we choose to imbue them with? Do you write your story from the perspective of someone who views difficulties as a chance to empower yourself?

Action

Forgive Having guilt or assigning blame to others can keep you firmly rooted in a past that cannot be changed. Identify what you need to release.

Find comfort Whether it's friends, family, or a cosy home, surround yourself with people or things that give you a feeling of safety. Although grief inevitably brings change, find solace in the things that have not changed.

Focus on what you can do What has been lost cannot be recovered, but concentrating on things within our power can make us feel less helpless.

Find your centre Examine the lessons of your hardships, and identify what has survived through each of them. Knowledge of what lies at your core, that which is indestructible, solid, and enduring, can help you have faith that you can and will overcome further obstacles.

Turn towards the future Think of how you can fortify yourself to deal with the future – put practical safeguards in place.

Turn obstacles into opportunities Every challenge is a chance to improve yourself. Consider how this one has strengthened you.

SIX OF CUPS

UPRIGHT
nostalgia · happy memories
renewing friendships
recovery

REVERSE
stagnation · no closure
trapped in the past
lost innocence

UPRIGHT

REVERSE

Interpretation

To heal from her wounds, the Fool seeks shelter from the present, revisiting the brighter moments of her past. Here, she finds refuge, comfort, and safety. This can take the form of fond memories, or even a physical homecoming. She may also be searching for answers and seeking closure. She gathers strength in these warm surroundings, but she must remember not to get lost in the past.

Happy memories can be restorative during challenging moments, but the Fool can't dwell within them forever and she must learn to adapt. She may cling to old memories in order to avoid the present. The past can bring lessons for the future, but that future depends on her living in the present, where she can effect change. Alternatively, this card may signal painful childhood memories.

Reflection

What do you miss from your past? What memories give you a feeling of contentment and security? They may be particularly comforting to you now, and can serve as guidance for the future. Can you connect with your inner child to look at the world with innocence and wonder? How would your inner child feel if they met you today?

Do your memories provide consolation, or are they distressing? Focusing on the past pulls us away from the present. Are you trapped in the past? Do you keep trying to revive happy memories that served their purpose, but have now run their course? Or are you haunted by old regrets that get in the way of you experiencing the full richness of life?

Action

Reconnect with the past Identify your fondest memories, and who or what figured strongly in them. Try to bring those elements into your present, whether it's through getting in touch with a long-lost friend, or picking up a forgotten childhood hobby.

Find simple pleasures In childhood we view the world with wonder and awe. Try to look at the present with the fresh eyes of your inner child. Name the little things in life that made you happy.

Seek closure Identify what is unresolved; observe the memories that you keep going back to and try to understand what you need to do to get closure.

Learn from the past Examine the lessons or coping mechanisms you learned from your past experiences. Observe whether these lessons are applied positively or negatively.

Draw a line If you find yourself being consistently drawn towards the past, make a separation between your present self and your past self. Don't let old wounds reopen and bleed into the future.

SEVEN OF CUPS

UPRIGHT
daydreaming · fantasy
decision fatigue
illusions

REVERSE
escapism · uncertainty
too much choice
overwhelmed

UPRIGHT

REVERSE

Interpretation

The Fool is offered a dazzling array of choices; some leading to fame, power, and wealth, and others to love, joy, and life's simple pleasures. Each has its own allure, so she finds herself lost in those daydreams, wishing and hoping without actually taking any action. She must truly know herself and apply a healthy dose of reason in order to turn fantasy into reality.

Choice can be wonderful, but when faced with too many options we can feel overwhelmed. Everything is an enticing distraction. Instead of making an active decision, the Fool may wait until a choice is made for her. Like its upright counterpart, there is an emphasis on fantasy and illusion here. However, reversed there is a stronger warning to make choices grounded in reality.

Reflection

Are endless options enticing and tempting you, seductive in their own way? Are you avoiding reality in lieu of pursuing some far-off fantasy? What daydreams do you have that allow you to remain dreaming without taking action? Can you turn your romantic, professional, or creative daydreams into an actionable plan?

An abundance of options can be an enviable situation or a nightmare of potential regrets. Are you paralysed by an overwhelming amount of choice? Do you retreat into your own world? Do you take the easiest route? In some extremes, this card can also point to a drug or alcohol problem. What choices are too painful or crushing for you?

Action

List the consequences Make a list of the best and worst possible outcomes. Understand what can be lost and gained with each choice. Don't let possibilities float disorganized in your head. Putting things down on paper makes them feel real.

Be realistic Identify paths you can actually work towards and follow them with passion.

Scale down your dreams It doesn't have to be an all or nothing affair; our dreams can come true, or at least a version of them. Identify how you can scale down dreams to make them more practical and achievable.

Be aware of warning signs Being cognisant of how you react when overwhelmed can help you see the signs before things worsen. Start planning when you feel this coming.

Give yourself a time limit Keep yourself accountable. Don't rush through decisions, but having a deadline can keep you focused.

Unmask anxieties Name your fears; uncover which of these are realistic and which are fabrications of your anxieties. Determine where your anxieties originate, and plan around those that are real.

EIGHT OF CUPS

UPRIGHT
walking away
difficult choices
withdrawal · abandonment

REVERSE
fear of change
denial · stagnation
avoidance

UPRIGHT

REVERSE

Interpretation

The Fool has surmounted the escapism of the seven, but she quickly finds that she has made the wrong choice. Originally, this path brought her happiness, so she invested herself whole-heartedly. However, she is disappointed at the outcome; regardless of how much she tries, she still feels empty. Though painful, she knows that she must leave it behind to find true happiness.

Reversed, the Fool attempts one more time to make an unfortunate situation better. The disappointments continue, and she may be losing hope. Still she finds it difficult to throw away something she has put so much effort into. She may feel less scared living an unfulfilling life that she knows, versus one that has the potential for true fulfilment but is full of unknowns.

Reflection

Life is a winding path; sometimes we must take steps backwards to move forward. What must you now leave behind in your career or personal life? Could walking away be for the greater good? It is not easy to leave something that is comfortable and familiar. What other difficult goodbyes have you said? Did doors open for you as a result?

What desires, dreams, and hopes do you repress in order to remain comfortable? What are you missing right now in love, your career, or elsewhere? Are you unable to leave your current unfulfilling circumstances? Starting over can seem more difficult than bearing the status quo for another day but denying your own happiness can be damaging long term.

Action

Say your goodbyes Be grateful for the time and memories that they gave you, but make peace with the fact that changes must come.

Embrace vulnerability Striking out on a new path will feel scary and uncomfortable. Let yourself feel this, and know that growing always comes from discomfort.

Follow your own star Your journey is one that is uniquely yours, with all its bumps and detours. Let your inner self be your guiding star, and find happiness in the twists and turns that come your way.

Know what you lose A slow decay can be sometimes more brutal than making a momentous change. Consider what more time in your current situation does to you. The longer you stay, the harder it may be to make a change in the future.

Address fears Examine what stops you from taking stock of your life and making the changes to find true happiness. Identify what you are scared of leaving behind, and what it is about your current situation that seems easier to ignore.

NINE OF CUPS

UPRIGHT

contentment · pleasure
tranquility · wishes fulfilled
comfort · satisfaction

REVERSE

disappointment · gloom
disheartened · unfulfilled
disillusioned

UPRIGHT

REVERSE

Interpretation

Known as the wish card, the Nine of Cups symbolizes deep appreciation and contentment. The Fool has found the peace that comes from having all of her needs and desires met. After the emotional upheavals of the cups, she has finally reached a calm satisfaction that allows her to enjoy her surroundings. Happiness is fleeting, but that knowledge only makes the present sweeter.

Reversed, the Fool has everything that she could have wished for. She could not have imagined a better outcome, but something does not feel right. She can't quite articulate why, but she feels emptiness. In her quest for happiness, she may have desired external markers of success, allowing status to dictate what she should pursue instead of allowing her heart to speak.

Reflection

Do you know what your emotional needs are? Are you experiencing the satisfaction that comes from knowing your wants, and pursuing them? When we discover our self-worth and take action from a place of love and respect, we find the secret to happiness. What have you always wished for, that you have right now?

You may have achieved many of your career or life goals, but this has not brought you true happiness. Are you experiencing feelings of emptiness, despite having all the trappings of success? Others may envy you, but are you restless? Do you look to others to understand what you should be achieving? What outer markers of success did you strive for?

Action

Be proud Embrace the fact that your dreams came true. Cherish them, enjoy them, and look back at the hard work you put in to achieve them. You can now inspire others to pursue their own dreams.

Make a wish Dream big; know what you would wish for, if you could have anything. Consider whether your wishes are aligned with your most authentic self.

Enjoy the moment Savour the gifts that life brings you. With feelings of gratitude and optimism, we open the door for more happiness to come.

Reassess your goals Consider why you choose to pursue your path. Identify the external factors that pushed you towards that choice, and whether you were living for someone else.

Put your ego aside Determine which goals were superficial. We all have egos, and sometimes we want the best things in life just to make others envious. Reconnect with what is important and see how your priorities shift.

Avoid excess You may be over-indulging in life's pleasures. Maintain a sense of balance as you enjoy its gifts.

TEN OF CUPS

UPRIGHT	**REVERSE**
family · home	domestic disputes
fulfilment · emotional security	dysfunctional family
fulfilling relationships	lack of community

UPRIGHT

REVERSE

Interpretation

When the self-love within the Ace of Cups overflows and nourishes all, we find true emotional fulfilment with community and relationships. The Fool's life is filled with loved ones. The connections represented by this card are deep, loyal, and harmonious. It signals a pleasant family life, but can also apply to romantic relationships, or the love and compassion within larger social circles.

In reverse, the familial and community bonds of this card may be weakened or twisted. Issues can arise at home or among social circles, creating distance, discontent, and friction. Appearances are deceiving; from the outside things may still look blissful, but there is turmoil within. In worst-case scenarios, there can be familial breakdowns, neglect, or even abuse.

Reflection

So much beauty and magic fills your life right now, and you can feel the gratitude deep inside you. This is the card of true belonging, of feeling loved and loving in return. Who are your strongest connections with? Who makes you feel unshakable, even in turbulent times? Who can catch you when you fall? Do you fully appreciate these relationships?

Is there trouble within your domestic situation or a relationship? Is your ideal picture of domestic bliss not matching reality? You may not be feeling supported, safe, and unconditionally loved. How does this affect your romantic life? What does it mean to feel at home? And how have your expectations not lined up with the truth of your situation?

Action

Cherish relationships Identify the relationships that give you a sense of safety, belonging, and unshakable confidence. Be grateful for these people who support you.

Connect with the idea of home Consider what the concept of home means to you. Examine whether it is a place, a person, or a feeling that comes with you in your heart.

Nourish connections Do something special for your loved ones. Bring a gift, cook a meal, plan a family trip. We often reserve these little gestures for special occasions, but we don't need an excuse to show love.

Recognize idealizations We often have unrealistic ideas of what it means to live happily ever after. When things don't live up to those ideals, we can be utterly disappointed. Identify any improbable expectations you have that may be causing your current feelings of disillusionment.

Redefine home Having no happy home to return to creates risk and frustration. Change your understanding of what it means to find a home, and learn to bring that feeling with you wherever you go, instead of depending on a physical manifestation.

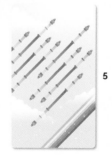

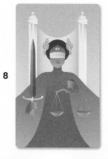

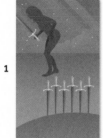

CONFLICT RESOLUTION

1 YOUR ROLE
Seven of Swords (see pp.170-171)

2 THEIR ROLE
Ten of Swords (see pp.176-177)

3 EXTERNAL FACTORS
Hermit (see pp.62-63)

4 WHAT TO IMPROVE
Seven of Wands
(see pp.106-107)

5 WHAT TO AVOID
Eight of Wands (see pp.108-109)

6 LESSON
Six of Pentacles Reversed
(see pp.198-199)

7 IS RESOLUTION WORTH IT?
Five of Pentacles (see pp.196-197)

8 ADVICE
Justice (see pp.66-67)

REAL-LIFE READING | Alyssa

A friend has been struggling with a work issue and asked Alyssa for guidance. However, Alyssa's advice has led to their friendship deteriorating. After another fight, Alyssa is consulting the tarot to help her understand the other side of the conflict. She is using the Conflict Resolution spread.

1 When first asked for advice, Alyssa was not initially forthcoming with her opinions, signalled by the **Seven of Swords**. Instead of confronting the issue honestly she felt it was better to be strategic, and even perhaps avoidant, with her words. This lack of clarity marked the start of the conflict.

2 The **Ten of Swords** indicates that her friend's worst nightmare may have come true. This card signals problems that have been building up for a long time, and an inability to escape fears, anxieties, and self-made prisons, culminating in dire situations. Similar issues have been following this friend from job to job, and a disagreement over the root cause of the problems has created the current tensions.

3 The **Hermit**, representing withdrawal and solitude, is Alyssa's default mode for dealing with conflict-laden relationships. This solitary time may also give her space to introspect and clear up how she wants to proceed with this situation.

4 The **Seven of Wands** signals that in order to improve the relationship, Alyssa must now make her intentions clear so that her friend understands her advice comes from a place of care and wanting to help, not out of a desire to hurt. Now that the relationship is strained, Alyssa must defend herself and stand up for her beliefs.

5 Alyssa must be careful not to react spontaneously, represented by the **Eight of Wands**. What is required now is a delicate touch. The emotional environment is one of tension, and if she behaves without sensitivity it may lead to more divisions.

6 The lesson she must learn is the **Six of Pentacles Reversed**; Alyssa needs to consider her reasons for giving advice. Are there control issues? Did she just want to be right? Was she fed up? When voicing her opinion, she must understand that even when asked for advice we can't expect others to necessarily accept or follow it.

7 Though Alyssa and her friend have been close, the friendship has been rocky, with their interactions becoming increasingly unpredictable. Most of the time Alyssa is anxious around her friend and feels she is walking on eggshells. She must consider whether she has the emotional resources to sustain this volatile relationship, depicted in the **Five of Pentacles**.

8 The best course of action is to act with magnanimity, fairness, and good faith, represented by **Justice**. This card also indicates the law of cause and effect; Alyssa may need to learn to trust that everyone learns the lessons that they need to in due time, and that attempting to interfere, even with the best intentions, can lead to trouble.

PAGE OF CUPS

UPRIGHT

inner child • messenger • shy
idealist • naive • sensitive
dreamer • imaginative

REVERSE

insecurity • rejection
criticism • gullible
sullen • wounded

UPRIGHT

REVERSE

Interpretation

The Page of Cups is our inner child, innocent and naive, whose imagination and daydreams often whisk her away from routine. She may seem absent-minded, lost in dreams. She is softly spoken and sensitive, interacting with the world with shy curiosity. In the realm of the arts is where she excels. There, she can translate her vivid internal life into expression.

Although this Page is gifted with a deep sensitivity, that same sensitivity can get her in trouble. She can use her imagination to escape life's troubles, or throw temper tantrums if reality becomes too much to bear. She suffers greatly when facing rejection or pain, more so than the other Pages. Her gullibility makes her vulnerable to those who would take advantage.

Reflection

When did you last enjoy total creativity and playfulness, and let your imagination run free? Your inner child wants to find delight in the wonder of your inner world. Can you give yourself more room to let your mind wander and your hands create? Do you worry about being perfect? Can you instead focus on expressing the total depth of your feelings?

Have you been emotionally wounded in your personal, professional, or romantic life? Rejection or criticism may have caused some shock, hitting your most tender spots. How does exclusion or judgment from others make you feel? There is also a sense of drama in this card – are hurtful words being felt more acutely than they are intended to?

Action

Create playfully Let your creativity run free! A child doesn't censor themselves, or think too much about whether the things they make are good enough. Let your imagination flow, and enjoy the process of creating.

Trust your inner voice This card also represents developing awareness of your inner world, and your intuition. Help that aspect of yourself flourish by following where it leads you.

Be open to surprises This is also the card of happy surprises. Opportunities may come along when you least expect; embrace them!

Let yourself heal Have a good cry, and let out the negative feelings. What feels like a wound that may never heal can sometimes be soothed by a moment of release.

Turn criticism into an opportunity Even when it hurts, take criticism constructively and you may find chances to improve.

Identify insecurities Self-doubt can magnify the slightest hint of displeasure into suffering. Examine your insecurities, and the feelings that arise when they are confronted. Knowing what they are can help you identify when feelings are disproportionate to reality.

KNIGHT OF CUPS

UPRIGHT
lover · seductive · chivalrous
moody · charmer · idealistic
poetic · romantic

REVERSE
vain · narcissistic · sulky
brooding · melodramatic
insecure

UPRIGHT

REVERSE

Interpretation

The Knight of Cups is romantic, sophisticated, and creative. He wants nothing more than to enjoy life's pleasures and make others happy. He is an appreciator of beauty in all forms, so he is often immaculately dressed, refined, and fashionable. He is open about his vulnerabilities, but often moody. He dislikes conflict and takes the role of peacekeeper or mediator during tense situations.

The Knight of Cups when reversed may allow the more negative aspects of his character to flourish – appreciation of beauty becomes vanity. Narcissism can also be a danger. He may be sensitive to criticism, weaponizing his emotions to create disharmony. When threatened with criticism or rejection, he may find it hard to confront them directly, and instead choose to be passive aggressive.

Reflection

Do you fall in love easily? Are you in love with the idea of being in love? Whether people or things, this Knight sees everything with a romantic eye. What pulls at your heart strings? Your feelings may be strong now, so express them. How do you show loved ones that you care? Do you naturally display your emotions, or are you shy?

How do you deal with feelings of inadequacy? You may be concerned too much with appearances and how others view you. Are you searching for validation? How do you want to be perceived at work, at home, or in your romantic life? This can be a time of deep vulnerability. Does every movement feel personal or like an attack?

Action

Appreciate beauty Open your eyes to what captivates you now. Not necessarily to aesthetics, but inner beauty. Explore what you find beautiful, poetic, or lyrical. Go to a museum, walk through a garden, surround yourself in things that delight you.

Dress to impress When it comes to appreciating beauty, apply this to yourself as well. Explore what makes you feel beautiful; wear the clothes that make you feel special.

Keep it light Try to avoid your darker emotions, and bring some of that Knight of Cups charm to your social interactions.

Be objective about emotions Beware of taking things too much to heart. When you are hurt, step back and take a careful look at what is actually being said, and the intentions of the person who said it. Try not to assume malicious intent, and take words at face value. Determine how doing this changes your experience.

Face conflict Examine what battles you are avoiding. Try being upfront about the issues at hand and see where it takes you.

QUEEN OF CUPS

UPRIGHT	REVERSE
emotional · loving · tender	gloom · melancholy
gentle · nurturing	depression · avoidance
supportive · creative	self-sacrifice

UPRIGHT

REVERSE

Interpretation

This Queen drifts back and forth between reality and her imagination. She has learned over time when she must be practical. She sees beauty where others do not. Many are drawn to her wisdom, for she is a good listener and understands people innately. She always gives others a shoulder to cry on, but her nurturing qualities can mean she takes on the emotional burdens of others too easily.

Reversed, this Queen drowns in the turbulent sea of her own emotions. She finds herself easily swept away by her feelings. The real world is too harsh so she remains in her own imagination rather than facing reality. Her moods are like the tides; fickle and erratic. Deep emotions coupled with worrisome circumstances can also make her insecure, needy, and clingy.

Reflection

Your depth of emotions gives you deeper insight into yourself and the human condition. What do your feelings show you? Are you more intuitively aware of others' needs now? Do you desire to comfort them? You may exude nurturing; your wisdom and the ability to see beauty in the ugliest of places makes you a sanctuary for those in need.

With her sensitive heart, this Queen cannot help but suffer when she sees people in pain. When you help others, can you stop yourself from being drawn into their negativity? Is it possible to relieve someone else's pain without feeling it yourself? If you are feeling overwhelmed with suffering, these emotions will need to be released.

Action

Be gentle Tap into your natural sense of empathy, and explore how you can best support others. Be sure to balance your own self-care and caring for others.

Make a difference If you've been touched by someone's plight, trauma, or tragedy, do something about it. Transform feelings into action, and make someone's day better.

Find your sanctuary You may have the role of listener and giver. Ensure that you have someone to turn to if you need it. Identify and seek out the people who can provide you with support.

Identify scarcities When we are lacking in love, we may feel weak and easily shaken. We can try to replace love with fantasy objects, or alcohol. Determine where in your life you feel empty and what wounds you are trying to heal.

Consider your sacrifices Contemplate whether you are denying your own needs in order to serve others. Being self-sacrificing can affect you in the long term. Too much self-denial is not sustainable, nor kind to yourself. Search for where you can make compromises.

KING OF CUPS

UPRIGHT

wise · compassionate
diplomatic · sincere · open
tolerant · meditative · calm

REVERSE

turbulent · repressed
wounded · bitter
uncaring · rage

UPRIGHT

REVERSE

Interpretation

This King's life was not always smooth sailing; the seas were sometimes gentle, and other times stormy. Through experience he found emotional balance, so that whether the tide rises or falls, he is centred. He is gentle, but not weak. He has mastered channelling emotions to maintain harmony and balance. He is a wonderful diplomat, easily able to empathize with many points of view.

In turbulent waters, this King can no longer remain afloat. He once knew how to direct the tides to always find stability, but now he is drowning. He may be dysfunctional, repressed, or completely lack emotion. If water is not allowed to flow, it becomes sick and stagnant; feelings are that way too. The Fool is cold and uses his knowledge of feelings to manipulate or exert dominance.

Reflection

Emotions are powerful – they can be destructive or harnessed for good. When they are a raging tide, can you direct them? Their strength may be fearsome, but can you channel your feelings into something constructive? Will you choose to act upon your emotions? How can you take what you are feeling now, and put it to productive use?

What happens to you when you feel flooded by negative emotions? You may find it difficult to remain calm right now, and your feelings could be strong and raw. Are you releasing your emotions in destructive ways? Do you let them build until you lash out? Do you hold them in and allow them to fester? How can you better cope with your feelings?

Action

Take a calm approach The King of Cups maintains composure through the most difficult of situations. Try to do the same, and become an anchor for everyone else.

See everyone's point of view If you're embroiled in a conflict, resolution can come through greater awareness of what each party's needs are. Try to find a resolution where everyone is considered.

Use your emotions Examine your current feelings, and what it would mean to put those feelings into practical use. Translate strong emotion into physical action.

Find release In moments of anger, find an outlet. Keeping negativity inside can turn toxic, but lashing out at others is cruel, too. Find ways to release your emotions that don't hurt others or yourself – scream in your room; punch a pillow; or put pen to paper.

Seek love in non-destructive ways When we are missing love, we unconsciously seek it. Consider if you have ever asked for love destructively; whether you've thrown a tantrum when you just wanted someone to show they cared. Try to be more honest about what your needs are.

ACE OF SWORDS

UPRIGHT	REVERSE
ideas · breakthrough	confusion · conflict
efficiency · discovery	hostility · obstacles
clarity · new perspective	miscommunication

UPRIGHT

REVERSE

Interpretation

The Ace of Swords can signal a breakthrough – a moment of extreme clarity that can change one's entire perspective. New doors are opened. The sword is a tool that cuts with a double-edged blade; it can be wielded to slice through uncertainty to find truth, or it can cause great suffering. Should the Fool grasp it, he must choose what to do with its power. Will he use it to destroy or to create?

Reversed, judgment is clouded and there may be confusion over what should be done next. Energy must now be spent searching for answers before pushing forward with plans. This card can also indicate that the sword is being used for brutality rather than truth. There can be needless conflicts, especially those that arise from lack of communication or a misunderstanding.

Reflection

Are you having a "Eureka!" moment, when all the pieces are coming together? Trivial matters are cleared away, revealing the core of what you need to know. Can you now find the initiative to get a personal, work, or creative project going? Are you approaching new plans with reason and logic? If so, success will surely follow.

Is confusion clouding your thoughts? How can you clear the air with a partner, family member, or colleague? What remains unspoken? Diverging expectations and interests may mean that discussions are needed. How can you approach these conversations with fairness and honesty to avoid unnecessary conflict?

Action

Find the essence Ensure your intentions are clear. Cut away all unnecessary details and complications and focus on facts and what needs to be done. This is the core of things.

Put pen to paper Seeing things written down can help create organization. Compile a to-do list of your tasks, but cross off everything that doesn't align with your main focus. See what falls away.

Take the initiative Plans that have been waiting in the wings are now ready to be hatched. Use the sharpness you have now to bring them to fruition. Take the plunge.

Spell it out If you felt something wasn't worth saying because it was obvious to you, don't let it remain ambiguous: say it. Being clear on your expectations and needs can be crucial now.

Search for truth If you don't understand something, ask. There's no shame in asking questions; especially if not knowing answers can lead to more trouble down the line.

Take another approach If a problem has been a consistent obstacle, it's time to take a different perspective. Your mindset may have been preventing you from solving this.

TWO OF SWORDS

UPRIGHT

avoidance · indecision
hesitation · reluctance
uncertainty

REVERSE

turmoil · disorder
stress · impasse
pressure

UPRIGHT

REVERSE

Interpretation

Difficult choices are marked by the Two of Swords. The Fool stands at a crossroads, and no matter which route she takes, the road ahead will be bumpy. Darkness hides the full circumstances surrounding this choice. Without information, she is indecisive. Even if facts are obvious, there may be denial or stalling, hoping that if she waits long enough the decision will be made for her.

Reversed, the stalemate is more painful, stressful, and overwhelming. Each direction contains much worry, anxiety, and pain. Every path has its own special brand of grief. There may be too much data to process, and making a choice now can create much inner turmoil. The longer the Fool waits, the more pressure there will be; the clock is ticking and sometimes any choice is better than none.

Reflection

How do you handle making difficult choices? What lies at the core of any indecision? Do you avoid choosing because either option will make someone unhappy? Do you believe the choices are mutually exclusive, and you fear losing possibilities? Is the responsibility of your choice overwhelming as it affects your family, your workplace, and more?

The time has passed for making logical decisions, and you may be cornered. Did you put off making a decision for too long? Are you now being forced to hastily choose? Procrastination often comes from anxiety – what do you fear? Can you challenge things head on before a boss, partner, or someone else makes a choice for you?

Action

Face your fears Be honest about what you're trying to avoid. There's no use pretending that the problem doesn't exist, or that it will just go away on its own if you leave it be.

Organize and analyse Banish the uncertainty as much as you can. Compile a spreadsheet, put together lists and see it all laid out. You may know more than you originally thought.

Investigate Do plenty of background research to gain all the knowledge you need to plough forward with a project. Get as much information as you need in order to feel comfortable with your decision.

Make a choice Time is running out. Sometimes making any choice will relieve you of pressure. Once a decision has been made, even if it's not perfect, you can focus on making the best of it.

Treat the underlying cause Identify what lies behind your procrastination and address it; you may be trying to avoid an emotion, or a worst-case outcome that is unlikely to occur.

Create a deadline You may not have all the desired information or confidence you had hoped for, but giving yourself a deadline will help focus the mind.

THREE OF SWORDS

UPRIGHT	**REVERSE**
heartbreak · separation	forgiveness · reconciliation
sorrow · suffering · grief	compromise · healing

UPRIGHT

REVERSE

Interpretation

Betrayal and suffering are marked by the Three of Swords. The heart is pierced with fierce words and angry actions, and the Fool may find himself more easily distressed by opinions or judgments. It is here where logic and objectivity will be helpful tools. What pain the heart bears, the mind sees with clarity, finds solutions, and knows that it will pass.

The momentary but intense suffering of the Three of Swords upright is now reversed, indicating that the Fool is beginning his recovery. The sorrow has not entirely ceased, but the clouds are parting. On the other hand, it can indicate that the Fool is having a hard time moving on from his heartbreak. He may be stuck in a period of self-pity, unable to see the possibility of a happy future ahead.

Reflection

The swords are the suit of communication, logic, and intellect. Have your wounds come from miscommunication, criticism, malicious gossip, or even the pain of realizing the cold, hard facts? How can you release these emotions – pull out the swords – to let your wounds heal? Can you let pain strengthen rather than diminish you?

In reverse, we see the swords dropping away from the heart, a vision of relief from pain. But it can also suggest internalizing sadness, or harbouring old wounds. What are you keeping locked up inside? Are these unspoken hurts festering and affecting your current relationships? What wounds do you still need to tend to?

Action

Speak to someone Words likely got you into this mess, and they can also help you out of it. Find someone you can trust, and let your grief flow out of you with words.

Focus on your strength Think of the heartbreaks you have survived and whether the pain lasted as long as you thought it would. Let your knowledge of these past wounds that healed soothe you now and make your suffering easier to bear.

Pause to find clarity Try to view the situation objectively and consider if it's really as bad as it seems. Perhaps it can teach you something.

Find a resolution With intense anger, calm discussion isn't possible. But now the door has opened for honest communication. There is a chance that everyone will have to bear some responsibility, as well as learn some lessons. Be prepared to forgive, and also own up to any mistakes or hurtful words you exchanged during heated discussions.

Seek help When we repress or hold onto past traumas, this can be difficult to solve on our own. Consider who can help you now – perhaps it's a trusted friend, a family member, or even a counsellor.

FOUR OF SWORDS

UPRIGHT	REVERSE
rest · recuperation	burnout · exhaustion
retreat · healing	collapse · self-neglect
preparation · sanctuary	stagnation · complacency

UPRIGHT

REVERSE

Interpretation

The Fool knows that she cannot go further without a time of retreat and recuperation. She has faced much pressure, grief, and sadness from a traumatic event or chronic stress. The Four of Swords is a time of healing, self-protection, and self-care. In the quiet of solitude, she finds sanctuary. She must conserve and replenish her energy to prepare for what comes next.

Reversed, the Fool finds exhaustion and burnout. Everything may be telling her that she needs to take a break, but still she resists. It can also indicate that a temporary rest has turned into passivity and stagnation. In her sanctuary, time doesn't stop – the world continues to place demands, but she may fear stepping back into the madness again.

Reflection

Stress arises from feeling that everything is urgent, which isn't always true. What stresses are you facing at work, home, or elsewhere? What do you need a break from? Without awareness of how we deal with stress, our bodies can force us to take a break. Life is a marathon, not a sprint. How can you treat yourself more kindly and guard your energy?

Are you being forced to take a break? What signs could you have heeded? Were others concerned with how hard you were pushing yourself? If you've instead struggled to bring yourself back into the world after recovery, you may still be in a vulnerable state. Can you find ways to be gentle, but also firm, with yourself?

Action

Ask for help If you're stressed about taking the break you need, find someone who can handle some of your responsibilities. Remind yourself that you are not alone.

Identify deadlines Deadlines help differentiate actual time-sensitive emergencies from other less urgent tasks and will encourage you to pace yourself.

Nourish yourself Find space in your busy schedule to set down a weekly self-care routine. Whether that means taking a long bubble bath or a walk through the woods, block that time out just for yourself.

Take a break Don't punish yourself for stepping away; not everything has to rely on you. Plus you are no use to anyone when drained. If you've been forced to take a break, let yourself rest. Others can step up.

Identify consequences When you push yourself too hard, the consequences are often worse than if you had paced yourself. Take notice of the effects of overworking.

Be proactive Change and conflict can be unnerving, but they can also be catalysts for growth. If you are frustrated with the stagnation in your life, take the lead.

FIVE OF SWORDS

UPRIGHT
bullying · deceit
hollow victory
intimidation · aggression

REVERSE
compromise · negotiation
losses · resolution
forgiveness · remorse

UPRIGHT

REVERSE

Interpretation

Aggression is suggested by the Five of Swords; there may be conflict, but no matter who comes out as the perceived winner, everyone loses. Sharp and painful words linger even when the fight is over. Ego may be at play here; some may feel that the most important thing is winning. Even if the Fool wins, trust and dignity has been lost. Every battle has its price.

Reversed, there is awareness that conflict leads to no progress. The Fool may have fought viciously, only to come out with scars and the knowledge that it was all for nothing. Instead of continuing the dispute, there is the desire to forget, forgive, and move on to something constructive. This card can also indicate escalating friction, despite one's best efforts to leave it behind.

Reflection

What does victory truly mean to you? Does it involve conquering others? Are there ways to win without hurting loved ones or others in the process? Does your victory necessitate another's loss? When we diminish others in order to lift ourselves, there is no true winner. This card calls for a careful understanding of how we treat others.

The way is now cleared for a temporary ceasefire, though feelings now may still be raw and hostile. Is there a willingness here for resolution, so that everyone can retain their dignity? What has been lost? How can these be lessons for future battles? Will more sacrifices be required from everyone in order to finally put an end to this conflict?

Action

Look at true costs Understand the consequences of your actions. While the adrenaline rush of being the victor may be tempting, what comes after may not be pleasant. Consider who you may regret hurting once all is said and done.

Apologize If you regret saying something that was unfair, there's still the possibility of reconciliation – ask for forgiveness.

Choose your battles All conflict takes its toll. Understand which battles are important to you, and ultimately serve your beliefs in the long run, and which to walk away from.

Listen The first step towards reconciliation is to understand other perspectives. We need to do this with openness; avoid being defensive. Listen and acknowledge the feelings that are involved.

Explore your remorse Take heed of the damage that has been done, and imagine what you could have done differently. Learn these lessons for the future.

Part ways Sometimes there can be no resolution, and the best that one can hope for is a clean cut. Perhaps the best choice is to move forward individually.

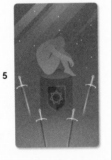

RELATIONSHIP DYNAMICS

1 SELF
Nine of Cups (see pp.142-143)

2 OTHER 1 (Sister)
Page of Cups (see pp.148-149)

3 OTHER 2 (Brother)
Ten of Wands (see pp.112-113)

4 RELATIONSHIP
Justice (see pp.66-67)

5 EXPECTATIONS
Four of Swords
(see pp.162-163)

6 STRENGTHS
Ace of Cups
(see pp.124-125)

7 WEAKNESSES
Two of Wands (see pp.96-97)

REAL-LIFE READING | Leon

Several years ago, Leon left his home country, where the remainder of his tight-knit family live. He asks the tarot how he can support his siblings from far away. He is using the Relationship Dynamics spread. Because there are two siblings, he has modified the spread by adding one more card.

1 The **Nine of Cups** is sometimes called the wish card, and here it signals that Leon has everything needed to feel happy. There is a sense of general satisfaction.

2 The sister is represented by the **Page of Cups**, who is sensitive, shy, imaginative, and naive. As the baby of the family, there is some worry about her moving away from her parents. She is similar to the absentminded dreamer this card represents.

3 Leon's brother, symbolized by the **Ten of Wands**, has just received a new medical diagnosis and may be struggling. Several things in his personal life have been difficult, and the problems are piling up to a point where it is no longer possible to carry the burden alone. This card can also indicate an unwillingness to share the emotional or mental burden. He may be quiet about his problems, but feeling them intensely. Perhaps Leon needs to ask his brother if he can help, instead of relying on his brother to come to him.

4 The relationship with siblings is seen as the **Justice** card; there is honesty and sincerity, alongside a strong sense of accountability. Everyone is reasonably responsible and emotionally independent.

5 The **Four of Swords** in the expectations position can indicate that Leon feels like his relationship with his siblings should be a refuge from the world. Their easy communication and frankness has made these relationships more open than the one he has with his parents.

6 The **Ace of Cups** in the strengths position signals that Leon's siblings provide each other with great emotional fulfilment. This ace can also mean emotional awakenings; Leon has realized relationships he took for granted before are definitely more cherished as distance is placed between them.

7 The **Two of Wands** as a weakness can indicate that the siblings are simply awful at making plans. While there is definitely love and support here, their independence and busy lives means that there is definitely room for improvement in communication. Leon may want to look at setting up monthly video calls, or planning their visits ahead of time.

SIX OF SWORDS

UPRIGHT
moving on · safety
shelter · relief
distance · transition

REVERSE
stuck · lingering
lack of closure · avoidance
resistance · paralysis

UPRIGHT

REVERSE

Interpretation

At the Six of Swords, the Fool bears great wounds and losses. The conflict in the Five of Swords proved to be very damaging, so she left in search of relief. She finds safety and calmer waters, though she could only bring what little she could salvage from the wreckage of her past. She may feel defeated, but knows that she must move on and transition to a new period in her life.

When reversed, instead of creating distance between herself and the past, the Fool chooses to head backwards. She may find it impossible to move on because of an unresolved conflict or a tense situation that she needs to find closure on. She may feel as though she is being forced to make a change that she doesn't want to; her situation makes her feel powerless or paralysed.

Reflection

There is a chance to start anew now, but the journey may be difficult. Are you moving on from your past professional or romantic life? Do you feel sadness, vulnerability, failure, exhaustion, or all of these emotions? Given the opportunity to start over, what would you want your future to look like? What mistakes can you avoid?

Are you searching for closure that is not possible at this time? Certainty is never guaranteed in life, and not all things can be wrapped up neatly. Can you make peace with the past by finding success elsewhere? Alternatively, are you running away from your problems? How can you turn around to face them?

Action

Learn from your emotions Negative feelings like sadness, grief, shame, failure, and loss give us context to live a meaningful and fulfilling life. Rather than trying to repress these emotions, accept them and then plan your movement away from them.

Don't let your past define you Let go of your past self. It is different from the one that you are nurturing and creating now. Think instead about the person that you would like to be. Grieve, and say goodbye to the aspects of yourself that are no longer aligned with your highest potential.

Make peace with uncertainty There may never be a reason for why things turned out the way they did. Going backwards in order to find answers will not make moving on any easier. When we relive the past, we also rekindle past injuries.

Embrace discomfort Discomfort is part of growing and experiencing new situations. The future changes that you need to make can be daunting, but that doesn't mean you have to run away from them. Let the knowledge of this be something that keeps you calm in uncomfortable situations.

SEVEN OF SWORDS

UPRIGHT
deception · strategy
tactics · cunning
resourcefulness

REVERSE
self-deception · malice
deviousness · secrets
conscience

UPRIGHT	REVERSE

Interpretation

Sneakiness and deception are at work here. You or someone in your life may resort to cunning strategies or work in secret for their own agenda. They may be lucky and get away with it, or get found out, leaving nothing but shame and guilt. On a more benign level, this card can suggest that resourcefulness and tactics are necessary. The Fool may need to be alert and clever to come out ahead.

Reversed, self-deception can be at work. Wanting something so much, the Fool may ignore all rationality and trick herself into believing a lie. An escalation of the upright situation is possible as well – there may be secrets, mind games, and layers of deceit that make it almost impossible to decipher the truth. This card reversed can also indicate a desire to free oneself from deceptions.

Reflection

Looks can be deceiving – is someone at work or at home putting on an act? Are you? When we have nothing to rely on except for our own resourcefulness, there is often no choice. Do you feel at a disadvantage? Cunning can be a survival instinct. Do you keep your secrets close to your chest? Your wiles could serve you well.

What lies do you tell about your romantic or professional self and why? Is there a convenient story you want to believe, a narrative that provides an escape from reality? Sometimes we want an easy way out so that we are not forced into taking action. What does it feel like to confront and reveal the truth – to yourself and others?

Action

Research Information is your best friend. The more prepared you can be, the better chance you have for success. Gather data, and put together a plan.

Keep quiet You may benefit from not sharing too much information. Try to be as self-sufficient as you can.

Use your position If you find yourself in the position of the underdog, you may have to act sneakily to persist. Others may not expect much from you, and you can use that to your advantage – they may not see it coming.

Come clean Eventually, the lies we tell ourselves and others can have grave consequences. You may need to confront the truth to prevent this from happening.

Unload secrets Over time, the secrets that we keep can build up, sometimes to a breaking point. Revealing the truth can be frightening, but can also bring great relief.

Tread carefully If you find that the environment of trickery has been escalating around you, be wary of manipulation and others trying to take advantage of the situation. Keep your wits about you.

EIGHT OF SWORDS

UPRIGHT
entrapment · self-victimization
imprisonment · restriction
negativity · self-sabotage

REVERSE
possibilities · freedom
release · optimism
resignation · denial

UPRIGHT

REVERSE

Interpretation

Surrounded, the Fool feels victimized, powerless, and trapped. She may be in a situation that feels inescapable. Her lack of agency makes her situation worse; she gives up any opportunity to make it better. What binds her is self-imposed. If she removes the blindfold that prevents her from recognizing her power and taking responsibility, she could escape this dire situation.

Reversed, the Fool's prison either gets narrower or expands to set her free. Maybe things are getting worse so that there truly are no options. Alternatively, the swords of this prison are loosening and falling away. The blindfold does too, allowing the Fool to see reality, without her fears and anxieties clouding her vision. She is now ready to take control of her life.

Reflection

Do you feel powerless? Are you waiting for someone or something to come and save you? Do circumstances at home, work, or elsewhere make you feel confined? This card can bring suffocating isolation, but also implies that you have everything you need in order to escape. What behaviours, attitudes, and beliefs are holding you back?

What beliefs, attitudes, and behaviours have you developed to cope with painful experiences? Do you believe that nobody will understand or love you? What are your prisons? Defence mechanisms can shape our lives until we no longer see the bars of the cell we have created. Can you remove your blindfold to fully experience your emotions?

Action

Take responsibility Self-victimization relieves you of taking responsibility for your life. Knowing that we are mostly responsible for the things that happen to us can be daunting, especially if we feel our lives aren't what we pictured them to be. Put aside pride and accept accountability; this can open the doors for you to build something truly yours.

Reclaim your personal power Identify who or what you give your personal power to. When we blame others, we also give them power over our lives. Focus on what you can do and make a plan to move forwards.

Enjoy your freedom When we find ourselves in control of our own lives again, it can be deeply fulfilling. List the things you will do when you reclaim your personal power.

Hold onto hope The hope that things will get better will be a powerful resource for you, even when releasing yourself is slow. Take pleasure in the little victories to retain a hopeful outlook.

Accept accountability Put your defences aside and take an honest review of your own mental restrictions. Examine what is really holding you back.

NINE OF SWORDS

UPRIGHT		REVERSE
worry · nightmares		trauma · despair
anxiety · fear		paranoia · escape
guilt · shame		self-hatred

UPRIGHT

REVERSE

Interpretation

If the Fool never released herself in the Eight of Swords, she then confronts the Nine. When the cold logic of the swords runs its course, an endless series of questions, worries, anxieties, and doubts can result. Nightmares run wild and the world feels inhospitable and ominous. She is haunted by the thought of what terrible events could be lurking around the corner.

This card can signify a recurring trauma that has not been resolved. The past may be haunting the Fool, and she may be spiralling towards despair. This card still brings hope that the reality is not as dire as one would believe. In a brief moment of clarity, she sees a way out of her misery, but she needs to muster all her courage and take steps to remove herself from this predicament.

Reflection

During the daytime, you may forget your worries because there are so many distractions. But when you lie down at night, what conversations or scenarios replay in your head? Does an off-hand comment by your partner turn into a fixation? In the quiet of night our minds can run in circles, tormenting us. What keeps you awake?

This card represents a pivotal moment, where either your fears can become worse or you can find a way out of your despair and torment. Who can give you support at this time? Concentrated effort on recovery and communication with others will be critical. Are your worst fears actually true? Who can help you separate reality from your anxiety?

Action

Crunch the numbers Compare the number of the things that you have worried about in your past with the amount that actually became real. Try to balance the terrible things that can happen with their likely chance of occurrence. See what falls away.

Find an anchor Before your anxiety spirals out of control, find something in the present that helps you hold onto the moment.

Find support Don't isolate yourself. Instead, get an outsider's perspective – find a friend or loved one you can talk to who can keep you grounded in reality.

Share your burden Problems we harbour in secret are exacerbated by the dark, but bringing them to light eases the load. Share your burden with a trusted person.

Find a therapist Sometimes, when this card points to trauma or worsening anxiety, we'll need professional help.

Choose hope With hope, we can interpret neutral situations positively and move towards resolution and healing. The path towards nihilism is led by fear. Don't lose faith; others can help you see hope in the dark.

TEN OF SWORDS

UPRIGHT
breakdown · defeat
failure · ruin
relief · closure

REVERSE
survival · transition
hope · release
endurance

UPRIGHT

REVERSE

Interpretation

Following the Fool on her journey through the swords, we could see her coming to a painful end. She has found herself in conflict and under stress. Unable to harness the sword's positive energy, she found herself tempted by its power. She was left with paranoia and fear, knowing that she had used the swords unwisely. Her fears were finally confirmed, leaving her defeated.

The swords pinning down the Fool are falling away, and the worries and stresses that have plagued her are easing. She hit rock bottom, but in her fall she has also found hope. The worst is now over, and she can focus on recovery. She has survived despite all odds, and she picks up the pieces to work towards a fresh start. The transition will not be easy, but there is light on the horizon.

Reflection

Has a problem that you have tried to outrun for so long finally caught up with you? Have your worst fears been realized? What situations at home or work are coming to a head? Has hitting rock bottom given you a sense of relief? Perhaps anxiety relents and you can now face your circumstance with certainty and a strange peace.

This card is tragic, but it also conveys that the struggle is over; there is nothing left to lose. What comes after will lead to a new beginning. Can suffering have a purpose? You have endured so much, but what did you learn? A part of you may have been lost here; how can you bury your ghosts and move forwards towards a fresh start?

Action

Face your worst fears Often when we confront our fears, even when we are forced to, they are not as bad as we had imagined. Compared with the constant state of anxiety, it may even be liberating. Take some comfort in no longer worrying about whether it can or can't happen.

Recognize lessons Consider all this a learning experience and take stock of your regrets. Think of what changes you would like to make once you have survived and healed from this ordeal.

Grieve To leave behind the past, we need to fully let it go. Say goodbye to the part of you that died here, and honour the lessons that this loss has taught you.

Separate Traditionally, burials are carried out so that what has died doesn't continue to haunt the living. In some ways, it's about making a fresh start. Draw a line between the past and your present and future.

Heal As your new beginning is on the horizon, focus on healing – nurture yourself. The dawn after the darkest night is coming; make sure you are ready for the journey.

PAGE OF SWORDS

UPRIGHT

curious · witty
quick thinker · chatty
alert · energetic

REVERSED

rude · insults
spiteful · manipulative
gossip · defensive

UPRIGHT

REVERSE

Interpretation

The Page of Swords is chatty and inquisitive, filled with nervous energy as she flits from place to place. She is a quick thinker and a great communicator. Her mind is fluid and adaptable, and her sharp sense of perception means she is always processing new information. She is honest, though sometimes tactless. Without focus, her mind can run around in circles and go off on tangents.

Reversed, the Page of Swords' mental agility may be used for more devious purposes. Her talent with words can inflict pain, whether covertly or upfront. She can make stinging remarks, creating trouble and rousing anger. She may gossip, turning people against one another. While this can be destructive, the Page of Swords may not even be completely aware of her detrimental behaviour.

Reflection

What fresh ideas and curiosities do you find yourself pondering every day? Now could be the moment to investigate them. Which of your creative or personal interests can you now research, learn from, or plan for? Your infectious excitement and curiosity may spark the interest of others. Where, or to whom, can your curiosity lead you?

Have you been lashing out? Feeling negatively about ourselves can make us project and inflict pain on others, even unintentionally. What in your personal, work, or romantic life makes you unhappy? Can you make a change for the better? Does a happier outlook on your own life make it easier to be happy for others?

Action

Be honest and direct Perhaps honest to a fault, this Page never minces words. She is not the type to spare feelings, but can be trusted to speak the truth. Now may be a good time to be open. Speak honestly.

Share your excitement This Page is animated and articulate; if you've found a new interest, share that excitement with others! Perhaps encourage them to join you.

Debate, don't argue You may find yourself more attracted to heated discussions lately. Engage that part of yourself, but be sure that they don't turn into more nasty disputes.

Think before you speak Maybe you're just someone who says it how it is. But when you hurt others with your biting words, you can lose friends and trust. Think of how you can deliver your message without causing anguish. Put yourself in their shoes.

Find the missing piece Look inwards and find where you are dissatisfied with your life. When we are unhappy, seeing good things happen to others can make us jealous or resentful. Don't deny yourself happiness, consider what you want, and seek it out.

KNIGHT OF SWORDS

UPRIGHT

determined · restless
focused · rebellious
swift · decisive

REVERSE

aggressive · hasty
rash · out of control
arrogant · bully

UPRIGHT

REVERSE

Interpretation

Being around the Knight of Swords feels like being in a whirlwind. He is full of energy and razor focused. He can be single-minded in pursuit of something, occasionally appearing ruthless. He is ready to take action and is easily bored when there is nothing to do. Always needing mental stimulation, he languishes without anywhere to channel his energy.

The Knight of Swords always walked a thin line between being extraordinarily focused and downright obsessive, so it is not surprising he has lost control. Reversed, he is a forceful bully and a know-it-all, lacking substance behind his words. Unable to admit that his hastiness has let him stumble into something that he doesn't understand, he may try to swindle his way to success.

Reflection

Where in your creative or professional life could you use a burst of energy? Your convictions, combined with external pressures, can be strong sources of power and movement. How can you better harness that power to create momentum? Do you deal well with intense pressure? Do you falter, or can you let it motivate you?

Good things take time. What happens when impatience is taken to extremes? Do shortcuts always work? We can suffer missteps and hurt others when we force something to go beyond its usual pace. Do you always need everything done now? Have you been disappointed when you rush? In what ways can you slow down?

Action

Go for it Don't waver, you should strike now. The time for thinking has passed, and swift action is now required.

Fight for what you want The Knight of Swords encourages you to carve out your own future. You may feel held back by others, but make sure you follow your convictions.

Stand up for yourself and others This card indicates you may be passionate and articulate when it comes to championing causes. Your strong feelings can now aid you, if they are directed in the right way and for constructive purposes.

Cultivate patience Think of the mistakes you've made in the past because you were hasty, and what could have been fixed if you were more conscientious. The journey towards the goal matters as much as the result. Learn to appreciate all the little steps you take along the way.

Keep an open mind The knight's beliefs are in danger of becoming rigid and fanatical. Focus can turn into dogma and ideology if not careful. Be open to opinions and constructive criticism from others – they can help balance you when you need it most.

QUEEN OF SWORDS

UPRIGHT	REVERSE
integrity · principles	critical · pessimist
perceptive · severe	bitter · grudges
aloof · truth	cruel · cold

UPRIGHT

REVERSE

Interpretation

The Queen of Swords is gifted with a nimble and perceptive mind, and nothing escapes her notice. She is strict but fair, though her detached and aloof air may intimidate others. For her, honesty above all is important; she always seeks the truth, even if it is painful. Her principles make her a powerful champion for her beliefs. She is guarded, but close friends will find a charming conversationalist.

Reversed, this Queen's intelligence is used as a weapon for bitterness. She may have been severely hurt in youth and is consumed by revenge, punishment, or hatred. Although her negativity is directed outwards, it is likely because she feels empty within. She may be excessively critical, never satisfied, draining, and toxic. Unwittingly, she causes the same suffering to others that she herself felt.

Reflection

How can we unite logic with feeling? When you have extreme emotions, can you just pause and try to observe them, as if observing another person? In the Queen of Swords, mind and heart come together as one. How can you apply logic to your feelings, so that you can channel them for the best possible outcome?

Yes, the world is full of terrible cruelty, but do beauty, kindness, and wonder co-exist beside it? Blocking out life's paradoxes makes us stagnant, sick, and weak. Do you believe that others only bring trouble and heartbreak? Without love, camaraderie, or friendship, hearts turn cold. What is the cost of being too guarded?

Action

Face the truth It is more important than ever to handle things with honesty, openness, and fairness. Regardless of how painful it can be, face up to any difficult truths.

Balance emotion with logic An awareness of feelings can aid communication and moral action. Let your words and actions come from empathy, but never stray from the truth.

Let your mind be free This Queen cherishes her personal freedom. New doors are open to her when she allows her mind to remain free. Keep an open mind and don't let the judgment of others restrict your outlook.

Let your guard down Not everything is a threat. The world isn't inherently evil. Don't nurse old wounds and let past suffering smother your chance for a happy future. Learn to trust again.

Don't assign blame Assuming malicious intent creates a cycle of negative actions and feelings. When we expect to be hurt, we act defensively, alienating others more. There is often a more benign explanation for others' behaviour. A bump from your colleague's chair doesn't have to be a declaration of war. It's more likely just clumsiness.

183

SELF-CARE

1 MY FEELINGS NOW
Knight of Swords (see pp.180-181)

2 SOOTHE
Nine of Pentacles (see pp.204-205)

3 ACCEPT
Ten of Wands (see pp.112-113)

4 ADAPT
Four of Wands (see pp.100-101)

5 WITHDRAW
Queen of Swords Reversed
(see pp.182-183)

6 EMBRACE
Temperance (see pp.72-73)

7 CELEBRATE
Death Reversed (see pp.70-71)

REAL-LIFE READING | Corina

Corina is coming to the tarot with an open mind, but doesn't quite have a question. She does feel a little "off", but there are no current big stressors in her life. She is looking for some general guidance from the tarot. She is using the Self-care spread.

1 Corina's current emotional environment is represented by the **Knight of Swords**, signalling a state of constant activity and speed. This card also suggests external pressures; life at work has been hectic, but it is in this kind of environment where there is the most excitement and energy.

2 The cards seem to indicate that Corina should take some moments to "treat herself", as represented by the **Nine of Pentacles**. Alongside the Knight of Swords, it seems to indicate that she is doing very well in her career, but perhaps could take more time to enjoy the rewards it brings.

3 The **Ten of Wands** signals that despite her protests and her denial, her hectic work life is a burden. She may handle it well, but it doesn't change the fact that this pace may not be sustainable long term. Even though it is her dream job, it can still be draining – and she must accept that these two paradoxical things can exist at once.

4 The **Four of Wands** at the adapt position seems to point to troubles at home, or within one's social circle. Corina moved to this city for work, but found it difficult to make friends, so instead of focusing on what was missing, her attention naturally focused on career instead. There may be a need to direct attention on life outside her career in order to create balance.

5 The cards indicate that she should separate herself from the **Queen of Swords Reversed**, which can either be an aspect of herself, or someone in her life. This person may be excessively critical and shaming. Corina admits she does have a tendency to judge herself too harshly. Some much-needed self-forgiveness may be what helps her to relax and enjoy the aspects of her life she has so far neglected.

6 Temperance should be embraced; as Corina develops more awareness of her inner needs, she can create a better balance between the different aspects of her life.

7 Finally, she should celebrate **Death Reversed**, a rather tricky card to have at this position. While it often signals avoiding change, it can sometimes indicate a self-initiated change, or smaller transformations. All the other cards seem to point towards change being needed; Corina can be the one, now with a more conscious understanding, to make it happen.

KING OF SWORDS

UPRIGHT
disciplined · stern
analytical · responsible
clear · logical

REVERSE
ruthless · inhumane
oppressive · brutal
controlling · violent

UPRIGHT

REVERSE

Interpretation

There is something formidable about the King of Swords. He carries himself in a way that seems restrained – carefully controlled and disciplined. He focuses on facts and figures, and there is a cold, calculating logic to everything that he does. He makes decisions guided by principles and strong morals, and is unflinching when dealing with challenging situations.

Without the King of Swords' intense discipline, we get his reversed counterpart. As he loses his self-control, he strives instead to gain control over others at all costs. He can be tyrannical, domineering, and ruthless. Upright, one could always trust that he would uphold his ethical values. Now he is callous and brutal; there is no sympathy or benevolence behind his cold nature.

Reflection

When is it okay to apply pure logic to a situation? When you create distance, do you make better or worse decisions? Can you look at your relationships, projects, and other aspects of your life with objectivity and detachment? This kind of discipline enables us to make choices that are fair, even if they are sometimes sad.

How do you respond to chaos? Is your approach to rules too rigid? Do you have a desire to be in control? When we seek to control our environment through force, it's usually because we see the freedom of others as a threat. Does your will and the will of your partner, loved one, or anyone else always have to be in conflict?

Action

Create order and rules This King excels in a world that is ordered, with clearly established rules. Set up an environment that matches those qualities. This can often create clarity.

Be direct and clear It's not the time to allow your feelings to get in the way. Be very clear about what your goals are, and voice them with confidence.

Find an advisor Look toward someone with this King's qualities if you don't have them yourself. Find someone you trust to give you logical and principled advice.

Revise your rules Examine the purpose of the rules that you set for yourself and others. Some of them may be there to protect you, but others may just exist to give you a sense of control in a chaotic world. Understand your true needs, and see if there are other ways to satisfy them.

Don't act from a desire to punish When your expectations are not met, it may be second nature to act out of revenge, or a desire to make the other party suffer. Think instead of what would be more productive. Use the King's logic for ethical purposes.

ACE OF PENTACLES

UPRIGHT
opportunity · gift
prize · abundance
manifestation · prosperity

REVERSE
missed chances
financial blocks
poor investments · loss

UPRIGHT

REVERSE

Interpretation

The Ace of Pentacles indicates fresh opportunities in the material world can be grasped and used wisely now. With planning and hard work, one can nourish this seed for long-lasting rewards and stability. This path will be long and arduous, and success requires patience and diligence. The Fool may be tempted to cut corners to speed up progress, but shortcuts will lead her astray.

When reversed, the potential for something meaningful and long-lasting is slipping through our fingers. Opportunities arise and disperse quickly, and unless the Fool acts now, this one may pass her by. She must be on guard against any unscrupulous deals that may sound too good to be true, considering commitments carefully, and slowly accumulating resources.

Reflection

What does it feel like to be and have enough? When we see our blessings we tend to interpret events in our life as opportunities rather than obstacles. How much do your material or professional circumstances affect your self-worth? Do you have feelings of inadequacy that prevent you from recognizing opportunities that come along?

Have you been offered a new job or project, but procrastinated so the chance slipped by you? Opportunities can come in flashes, and we need to be prepared to seize them. Where do your hesitations stem from? Are there red flags, or is it based on anxiety? Decisions have to be swift, but also precise and methodical.

Action

Seek out opportunity While the world presents us with many chances to bring our plans to fruition, we must put in the effort. Search for fertile ground in different areas of your life.

Believe in your sufficiency When we feel ready, able, and strong, we can take on any challenge that comes our way. Trust in your own strength, and seek out new projects.

Nurture your seeds Without attentive care, chances can slip away. Identify what opportunities you've been given, and tend to them.

Check the details If your gut is telling you something is not right, be sure to check the fine print. Know what you are getting into.

Put together a budget Whether it's for a project, a rainy day fund, or simply for a better lifestyle, being conscientious of where your resources go can help create a better relationship with your finances.

Evaluate risk Account for the downside, and be prepared for what happens in the worst-case scenario. Know upfront about what risks you can tolerate in proportion to the potential rewards.

TWO OF PENTACLES

UPRIGHT	REVERSE
maintaining balance	burdens · imbalance
cycling energy	spread too thinly
flowing · resources	overwhelmed

UPRIGHT

REVERSE

Interpretation

Resources come and go, and though pentacles keep being exchanged, the Fool always seems to have two. There is balance here; these exchanges create a dynamic, but harmonic, equilibrium. With her knowledge of value, she can create momentum and grow her pentacles. She may feel overstretched now, but she will be rewarded over time if she masters balancing this material energy.

When reversed, the balance of material energy is upturned, and the Fool has spread herself too thinly. Responsibilities may demand too much, and she can't meet all of her commitments. There are not enough resources – money, time, or effort – to keep up with this state of affairs. She may put too much energy into one aspect of her life to the detriment of others.

Reflection

How do you manage your resources? What do you do when you have many commitments and responsibilities but very little time, energy, or finances? Life always seems to pull us in many directions. You can acknowledge all these pulls, but how can you prioritize? What do you value the most?

What prevents you from slowing down? Do you feel like you constantly have to take on more to pursue some ideal? You may be trying to juggle a career, dating, family, education, and more, while slowly wearing yourself out. How can you regain balance? You are not an infinite resource, and eventually you'll need to recharge.

Action

Observe nature She is the ultimate guide to dynamic balance. She constantly transforms energy and matter; no energy is wasted. She trades sunlight for leaves, decaying carcasses for new life. Flowers give nectar to butterflies, while butterflies give the flowers the possibility for reproduction. Everything finds equilibrium.

Balance needs Balance and harmony come from making sure that your needs and the needs of someone else are both met. Through this, we find a healthy exchange of giving and receiving.

Nourish yourself Now is the time to identify or find something that nourishes you, and gives you energy. These are the things that will keep you afloat in turbulent waters.

Rethink priorities Identify aspects of your life that you have neglected recently, and assess whether you are happy to sacrifice them in your pursuit of something else. You can't have your cake and eat it – this is not sustainable. Knowing and accepting that you must trade one aspect of your life for another is all part of the balancing act.

THREE OF PENTACLES

UPRIGHT
collaboration · growth
teamwork · organization
building foundations

REVERSE
competition · ego
lack of vision
discord · divergence

UPRIGHT

REVERSE

Interpretation

When the Fool reaches the Three of Pentacles, she sees that others are struggling too, and she has a brilliant idea. What if she were to work together with them? Though everyone is capable alone, this card embodies the lesson that the best things are not built in isolation, but with the collaboration of many people with different outlooks and skillsets.

Lack of teamwork and disagreements are marked by this card in reverse. There may be no organization, differing visions, or diverging expectations about each person's responsibilities. Sometimes, egos may come into the picture; perhaps one team member is more concerned with power and superiority than the project itself. All of this can push the Fool to work solo.

Reflection

When others appreciate your skills and talents, how does that feel? Do you work with people who value your expertise? If not, can you find professional or creative collaborators who will give you the space to flourish by doing what you do best? When you work with teammates, how can you best create that same kind of environment for them?

Do you hoard all the responsibilities to yourself at work or at home? Or do you end up micromanaging your peers? How does relying on other people make you feel? Are you reluctant to do so? Being entirely self-sufficient in order to avoid inevitable disappointments or to maintain control closes us off from others.

Action

Cultivate trust Working with others is all about letting go of some control, and trusting the other person to make the best choices. When we have difficulty collaborating with others, it can point to a fear of risk. Get comfortable with this fear, and believe in others' skills and abilities.

Know what you lack Knowing oneself is always the foundation for building better relationships. Know which personal qualities complement yours, and search for others who have them. Together, you are strong.

Hone a collective vision Find what unites all of you, and what is at the core of everyone's goals. Remaining dedicated to the common cause can help diffuse any one individual's desire to control a project.

Accept constructive criticism Respect that others have differing specializations that can bring new perspectives to the project or creation.

Find or be a leader When everyone resorts to bickering, there's usually the need for one person to be the voice that pulls everything together.

FOUR OF PENTACLES

UPRIGHT
stability · ownership
conservatism · caution
accumulation · fear of risk

REVERSE
spending · miserliness
greed · hoarding
materialism

UPRIGHT

REVERSE

Interpretation

With enough luck and initiative the Fool finds herself in a period of plenty. This was not easy, and she made many sacrifices to save and pinch pennies. She clutches her pentacles, finding comfort in them. But she also feels dependent, and when she obtains more opportunities and chances she finds herself unable to take them. She fears scarcity; perhaps she will never have enough.

Reversed, this card represents differing extremes – either over-generosity or excessive possessiveness and greed. The Fool is putting her resources to use; she may take more chances, and explore new things that she once rejected because she feared loss. But this card can also indicate growing hoarding tendencies. Reliance on material resources for stability turns to dependency.

Reflection

Have you ever clung to something, only to see it fall away? Sometimes we must learn to let things flow. What are you scared of losing? Why do you hold on so tightly? Ironically, when we cling desperately to something, we pull it out of its natural cycle, and our worst fears can come true. Have you ever met a clingy person? How did you feel?

Do you sacrifice today's happiness for greater happiness in the future? What elements of your personal, creative, or professional life can you enjoy now? Do you remember your original goals? When you accumulate without purpose, numbers can lose meaning. What does having more protect you from? What is enough?

Action

Identify insecurities Explore what makes you feel unstable and unsafe, and recognize the detrimental things you hold on to in order to avoid those feelings.

Identify symbols Sometimes we may use physical possessions to define ourselves. They often stand for status, power, success, or comfort. Learn to let go of these.

Look within Search for ways of satisfying your needs without objects. For example, success and money are not the same thing; we can have success without superficial signals.

Find release Even the most diligent of savers need to congratulate themselves with little rewards every now and then. Give yourself room to enjoy and put your hard earned resources to use.

Create concrete goals If you've been stocking up to feel secure, know that without an actual figure you may never feel like there is an end. Concrete goals are healthy because they can be measured, unlike feelings. Give yourself a number you need to reach or retain in order to feel safe, and hold yourself to it.

FIVE OF PENTACLES

UPRIGHT
instability · scarcity
material insecurity · loss
struggle · deprivation

REVERSE
improving circumstances
stability · realizing value
building resources

UPRIGHT

REVERSE

Interpretation

At the Five of Pentacles, the Fool's circumstances have greatly changed. He lost sight of the true value of things and is now destitute. Perhaps he spent too much time accumulating wealth instead of developing relationships. These would have been helpful for him now, but instead he feels alone. If he could only lose his self-pity and pride, he could see that others can help him.

Reversed, the scarcity of this card is lightened, and the Fool may be putting his life back together again. His experience of struggle may give him a new outlook. The unpredictability of life shakes him from feeling permanently lacking; he has experienced what it means to have nothing, and though it has been humbling, it has not broken him.

Reflection

Do you accept help when it's offered from colleagues, your partner, friends, or family? Or do you find it uncomfortable? Can you explore this discomfort? Sometimes, familiar things seem less frightening than trying something new and potentially flourishing. What is it that holds you back from seeking help and getting out of this difficult situation?

Have you ever lost something that you thought you needed, only to find out that you were fine without it? How would you feel if you lost all your material possessions? In some ways, losing what we thought were our anchors in life can be a blessing. What can your loss teach you about letting go and finding strength within?

Action

Find support Now is the time to swallow your pride and search for help. When we ask, we receive.

Understand what you need Being clear about how others can help you will make them more willing to step up. Having expectations without being able to define what they are only causes disappointment.

Know what you have Although material possessions come and go, there are things that last, and truly matter. Let this difficult period help you find what is indestructible in you and what can never be lost.

Embrace empathy Times of struggle can be powerful in increasing our empathy towards others who are in similar positions.

Reconsider value Understand what truly matters to you. When faced with loss, we can learn that what we thought would bring us happiness doesn't matter after all. See how your values have shifted.

Build resources Prepare for the future. Whether it's a stash of emergency supplies, strong community relationships, or finances, assemble things that can provide comfort during uncertain times.

SIX OF PENTACLES

UPRIGHT	REVERSE
generosity · charity	power dynamics
sharing · gifts	superiority · strings attached
assistance · support	abuse of power

UPRIGHT

REVERSE

Interpretation

This is the card of generosity and charity during moments of great need. This story has two different perspectives – those of giver and receiver. In a moment of desperation, the Fool searched for help and found a benefactor. Or she can be the giver; overcoming adversity, she has learned in her moment of scarcity that one person's help could make all the difference.

Reversed, this card can indicate uneven power dynamics, and giving that happens for all the wrong reasons. The relationship between the giver and the receiver can be tainted and motivations may be less than pure. Perhaps the giving is done to bolster the ego or retain control of the receiver. The receiver may be dealing with humiliation, resentment, and powerlessness.

Reflection

This card asks us to examine our feelings towards gifts. What do you have to give? What are you looking to receive? Whether it is material goods, emotional gifts, or the gift of time, how does both giving and receiving affect you? Are you uncomfortable when receiving? Where does that stem from and what assumptions are you making?

When you give something to others, are your intentions pure? Sometimes, power dynamics are in play. Do you give out of a desire to control? Do you give because of your own guilt, or to induce guilt in another? No exchange is ever purely material, it comes with its own emotional weight. If you're receiving gifts, are there any red flags?

Action

Know your limits If you're the giver, be honest with yourself about your boundaries. It's the best way to make sure you avoid resentment, preserve your own energy, and keep pure intentions. Know when to say no.

Pay it forward If you're the receiver, look on these moments with gratitude, and without shame or guilt. Make a commitment to help others in need when you have plenty.

Examine feelings When you feel shame and guilt receiving help, you turn giving and receiving into painful experiences. Explore the reasons why.

Understand your intentions If you're the giver, examine your true expectations. Giving is best when we just want others to be happy. But we can also give for a sense of control or power. If your motives are unclear to you, it is perhaps better to hold back.

A gift is a gift If you've been on the receiving end of both gifts and guilt trips, remind yourself and the giver that they chose to give this to you. It may be healthier to find someone who can provide help without judging or holding it over you.

SEVEN OF PENTACLES

UPRIGHT
harvest · hard work
slow results
long-term rewards

REVERSE
no rewards · impatience
waste · laziness
procrastination

UPRIGHT

REVERSE

Interpretation

The Fool uses the generosity from the six to put all her effort into developing something. For a while, she felt she was wasting her effort – progress was slow. With patience, her seeds have flourished into a large plant, heavy with fruit. Being so focused on the labour, she never took the time to observe the blooms. Finally taking a break, she gazes in awe at her creation.

Impatience may be an issue in the reversed Seven of Pentacles. No matter how much effort the Fool spends, there are few rewards. She may have to examine closely where her resources are going, and perhaps divert them appropriately. This card can also indicate laziness and procrastination. She may start many projects without ever completing them, giving up at the slightest sign of trouble.

Reflection

Do you want to do something that feels too daunting? Think of recent professional, creative, or personal achievements that you nearly gave up on because they they were so much work. Were you ever frustrated with your progress? Did you feel like you would never make it? How does your perspective change now that you've accomplished them?

What does progress mean to you? Is it outwardly visible, or more subtle? How do you measure it? We can improve our life little by little without seeing obvious outward changes. Sometimes progress means nurturing a new way of thinking. Sometimes it can be accepting that change comes slowly. How can you develop your patience?

Action

Evaluate your accomplishments As you push forward with your goals, take time to appreciate everything that you've worked so hard for. Be proud of what you've achieved.

Look for signs of progress Don't minimize your achievements. Find three things that are evidence of how much you've grown or progressed with your current project.

Reward yourself Even the smallest things are worth being happy about and celebrating. Keep yourself motivated with positive reinforcement. Give yourself a pat on the back!

Redefine progress Sometimes, we can get fixated on other people's markers of progress. This only magnifies setbacks when they happen. Measure your own progress by identifying what matters to you most.

Analyse and refocus Use a trial and error approach. See what worked and what didn't. Focus your energy on what provided results, and reduce the time you invest in what didn't.

Distinguish Knowing when to change direction and when to push through is a fine art. Follow your instincts, but validate them with facts, figures, and objectivity.

EIGHT OF PENTACLES

UPRIGHT
expertise · talent
commitment · excellence
craftsmanship · ambition

REVERSE
disinterest · poor quality
mediocrity · haste
unprofessional

UPRIGHT

REVERSE

Interpretation

Deep in concentration, the Fool is crafting something truly perfect. We see devotion and commitment to his creation, as well as contentedness. His is a labour of love. After a long search, he found his true purpose, and he gradually mastered his job. Even with his excellence, he still remains curious and excited to learn new techniques, knowing that true mastery always requires curiosity.

Without dedication, the Fool becomes disheartened and lazy. He makes a half-hearted effort to fulfil a responsibility. His love of his craft is gone, and it shows. He toils because he must; he needs to make a living. He may be blinded by the profit, so he does the job but cuts corners. Perhaps this was once a passion that died out. Outwardly he looks successful, but he lacks enthusiasm.

Reflection

Have you ever re-read a book or a poem, only to find new meanings? When we commit and dedicate ourselves to something, like a skill or a career, no work feels monotonous. Can you find joy in truly devoting yourself to something? How can repetitive tasks bring contentment? Here we find alignment between the material and the spiritual.

How do passions wane and turn into burdens? Re-examine your purpose and calling. When our passions turn into responsibilities, dread and procrastination can creep in. What is the true value of your role at work or at home? What do you do that improves lives? What do you do that makes others happy?

Action

Stay humble When you approach something with the expectation to learn, you can always find delight. When we stop being curious, believing that we know best and there is nothing left to learn, we never reach the heights we aspire to.

Find pleasure in the work Learn to enjoy the process, not just the rewards. Relish the satisfaction of getting things just right.

Cultivate your interests Mingle with others in the same line of work as you, take a class, research new techniques – these are ways to find inspiration to take you to the next level.

Delegate All work has aspects that you find unfulfilling. You may have more success if others can help take those aspects over, while you focus on your passions and what you do best.

Remember you're appreciated Spend time with people who value you. Re-read an uplifting thank you letter from a friend or a congratulatory email from your boss. Remind yourself of how you create positivity.

Take a rest If all else fails, coming back after a break with fresh eyes and renewed energy can change the way you perceive your work.

NINE OF PENTACLES

UPRIGHT

achievement · success
prosperity · flourishing
comfort · resourcefulness

REVERSE

superficial success
debts · tackiness
transactional relationships

UPRIGHT

REVERSE

Interpretation

Should the Fool remain diligent, she will find herself in the Nine of Pentacles, where she can finally relax and enjoy the fruits of her labour. Her journey has not been easy. She had to be dedicated, resourceful, patient, and even give up basic comforts. Her rewards have been hard earned. There are no real stresses for her right now; she enjoys the freedom and pleasure she worked for.

Reversed, the Fool sinks into debt as she surrounds herself with markers of stability and accomplishment. She may feel pressure to keep up appearances and maintain a lifestyle that gives her status, without the actual resources. Or she may have a hard time leaving work behind. Her relationships can be transactional and she forgets how to relate to others on a personal level.

Reflection

If you had everything you ever wanted, would you feel content, isolated, or bored? Do you enjoy your success? Some of us may feel shame and guilt about our accomplishments. Can you instead learn to just enjoy and take pleasure in the things that you have earned? Now is the time to sit back, relax, and enjoy your flourishing prosperity.

What lifestyle have you become accustomed to? When surrounded by luxuries, it can be hard to let go. Can you treat yourself without over-stretching? If this doesn't describe you, consider how the transactional nature of work follows you out of your workplace. How have you started to view relationships? With success, do you feel you have more to lose?

Action

Create your own space We are often deeply tied to our environment, and giving ourselves a space where we can feel comfort and relaxation helps us flourish. Decorate, hang new art, surround yourself with positivity.

Enjoy a slower pace of life When we achieve our goals, the pressure to strive and prove ourselves can disappear, making room for other things in our life. If you've denied yourself comforts and pleasures in the past as you worked towards your goal, try to indulge them now. There's no need to keep being so strict with yourself.

Separate needs from wants Pare down. Understand what are true needs versus objects that are substitutes for an emotional need. Find other ways to fill emotional voids.

Accept your humanity If failure seems more frightening now than ever, accept that it is human. We may always feel like we have to do better, go further, and that our future achievements must be greater than our past, but that can't always be. You may hold yourself to impossible standards. Let yourself be human, vulnerable, and scared, and forgive yourself for being so.

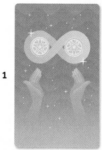

DREAM INTERPRETATION

1 DREAMER
Two of Pentacles (see pp.190–191)

2 THEME
Queen of Swords Reversed
(see pp.182–183)

3 CONNECTED EVENT
Four of Wands Reversed
(see pp.100–101)

4 WHAT IS REPRESSED
Devil (see pp.74–75)

5 LESSON
Knight of Swords (see pp.180–181)

REAL-LIFE READING | Jen

Jen is seeking a tarot reading because she is convinced that she is being followed by bad luck, with difficulties in her family, financial, and emotional life. She believes that it started two years ago with a particularly intense nightmare in which she was "cursed", so the Dream Interpretation spread was used.

1 The dreamer, Jen, is represented by the **Two of Pentacles**, indicating that her dream role was to create balance between competing needs, wants, and desires. This card can also signal that there is a lack of resources, requiring lots of careful balancing. There can be the feeling of one false move being enough to make everything fall apart.

2 The theme of the dream was the **Queen of Swords Reversed**, who can either represent Jen or another person in Jen's life. The main person in her dream was a shadowy figure, in front of which she felt oppressed. Upright, this queen is able to balance both emotions and logic. Following the theme of balance with the Two of Pentacles in the dreamer position, this card may represent Jen herself. She may search for ways to honour and unite her logical mind and her emotional self, but may fail to do so. This queen also represents someone whose stunted and repressed emotions cause her to create suffering for those around her. She may be this way because of past traumas, unwittingly lashing out because this is the only way she knows how to express her pain. She may need the help of an experienced therapist.

3 The connected event is represented by the **Four of Wands Reversed**, indicating that troubles in Jen's family life, or their immediate social circle, was the core issue. It may stem from a feeling of not having a home – a place of belonging, unconditional support, and safety.

4 The **Devil** is in the repressed position, indicating that there is something that occurred here that Jen is ashamed of, and instead of confronting it she has decided instead to ignore it and push it away. Jen must learn to accept this instead of restraining it. This card can be associated with addiction; whether it points to a physical substance, an emotion, or a narrative. The addictive nature of the card may correlate with being trapped in her dream. This card also ties into the idea that the shadowy figure in her dream may be an aspect of herself that she tries to repress. The Devil, after all, does represent our collective shadow-selves.

5 An upright **Knight of Swords** in the lesson position can be representative of our hero archetype that Jen needs to embody. He is swift, decisive, and active when confronting challenges. As a swords card, he uses his intellect when faced with murky emotions, cutting away extraneous details so we can see the truth.

TEN OF PENTACLES

UPRIGHT
permanence · legacy
ambition · family values
ancestors · honour

REVERSE
family conflicts
financial loss · materialism
family burdens

UPRIGHT	REVERSE

Interpretation

We find the Fool with her family at what is now her estate. She has built this little kingdom for herself and her loved ones. She feels content and safe, knowing that her hard work and sacrifice have been worth it. The walls are sturdy and will last generations. Her resources are now focused on supporting her family; she wishes her child never to go through the same harsh times she has.

Reversed, this card may signal issues regarding family, family money, honour, expectations, and traditions. There may be generational conflicts – freedom conflicting with familial expectations. A choice must be made between becoming self-reliant and succumbing to pressure. There may also be excessive focus on short-term results to the detriment of sustained future success.

Reflection

Consider the long-term impact of your actions – professionally, creatively, and personally. What do you want your legacy to be? What are your values, and how do you bring them out into the world? What do you want to be remembered for? We will live on in the memories of those that come after and the world that remains.

As we attain more things, material or spiritual, we also have more to lose. Do you think that having everything you ever wanted would allow you to live in perfect contentment? Remember it also opens the way for disappointment and fear. Can you live with this fear? Is it something to be dreaded? Or is it just the price to pay for success?

Action

Build foundations Work on something that will leave a lasting impression. Consider your values, principles, and purpose. Do small things that help shape the world accordingly.

Let love guide you One of our greatest legacies will always be love. Consider what you can do to foster that love. Build connections, work on your relationships, and forgive petty arguments.

Honour the past Seek out your elders, and learn from them. Find a family member or a mentor that can give you wisdom for a lasting future.

Follow your values Let the upright version of this card be a guide for how to live your life. Build something that is long lasting, as well as aligned with your individual principles. Sometimes, this means breaking with family tradition, leaving what is safe, and striking out on your own.

Find the source Our discomfort with success can come from imposter syndrome or low self-worth. Many successful people feel like they don't know what they're doing; you're not alone. By letting yourself feel the discomfort, it gets easier every day.

PAGE OF PENTACLES

UPRIGHT

academic · practical
studious · disciplined
loyal · dependable

REVERSE

uncommitted · lazy
undisciplined
no ambition

UPRIGHT

REVERSE

Interpretation

The Page of Pentacles is ambitious and practical, setting her sights on long-term goals that require much work. Her dedication will see her through challenges that others may find tedious or impossible. Sometimes she is rather stubborn, and her studious nature means she is easily teased. But she is also a warm, humorous, and helpful individual who makes for a great friend.

Reversed, this Page can be lazy and materialistic, setting high goals without putting effort into attaining them. Focused on the outcomes, she is easily swayed by schemes and shortcuts, and is often too restless and hasty to look carefully through details, which can get her in trouble. She may be lost in daydreaming, never carrying through with anything practical.

Reflection

What are you dedicated to? What drives you? Having something that you can devote yourself to can help guide you through life. Is it something concrete, a principle, or a purpose? Life is full of wayward paths where we can get lost, or they may lead us to harm. Knowing your guiding star can make that journey less confusing.

Are you feeling bored or burnt-out? How has that affected your professional or personal projects? You may have started out with passion, perhaps even turned a hobby into a career. But that comes with its own degree of sacrifice – does everything you do now have to be "productive"? What do we lose when we stop doing something for joy?

Action

Find your compass When we have a purpose, spending effort and energy comes naturally. Find something you can offer that the world needs. Find your inner compass, and act on what matters.

Set high standards This Page doesn't just want to do something, she wants to do it well. Hold yourself to a level of excellence.

Make a commitment Dedicating yourself means giving it your all, and not giving up when things get tough. Expect obstacles, challenges, and conflicts, but with enough willpower, you can succeed.

Reconnect with your passion Take a break and do something that makes you happy. Notice what changes occur when you do something for love versus usefulness. Notice how your outlook shifts.

Find inspiration Being around interesting ideas, people, and environments related to your original interests can be a reminder of what you loved so much. Creativity doesn't happen in isolation.

Focus Try to avoid distractions. Discipline is important now. When distractions do crop up to make you stray, focus on what is important.

KNIGHT OF PENTACLES

UPRIGHT
patient · skilled
responsible · honest
guarded · cautious

REVERSE
workaholic · selfish
cheap · routine
bored

UPRIGHT

REVERSE

Interpretation

Other Knights charge into new adventures, but this Knight stays at home, working his land. He always had a clear idea of what he wanted, and little by little, he has achieved small milestones. Others suggest new methods but, being stubborn, he chooses to rely on the tried and true. He may be shy and cautious about revealing his feelings, but he is honest, reliable, loyal, and trustworthy.

In reverse, this Knight's obsession with work can increase. He may neglect other areas of his life, which are easily sacrificed for his goals. He may be obsessed with attaining and owning, using material things as compensation for failures. Or he may feel bored and dull, like his life is an endless routine without meaning. Something must change, but fear of change paralyses him.

Reflection

Success in anything is hard earned, and you know this. Have you experienced struggle, sacrifice, and even failure? Are you able to grit your teeth and pick yourself up? It is difficult to appreciate the challenging times in the same way that we relish the moments of elation and pride when things go well, but can you learn to love the journey too?

What makes you feel lazy? What makes all of your hard work seem pointless? Do you feel like you're doing monotonous work without seeing results? When we see others' success, we rarely see the dedication, the boring routines, the late nights at work, the conflicts between lovers, and the repetition that is required to get there.

Action

Let discomfort motivate Growing always feels uncomfortable. Remember this when you feel like giving up. Let yourself feel that discomfort, but keep going through it, and slowly things will get easier.

Appreciate the journey Life is more than the result of your successes and failures. It is the experiences we have along the way. Value the lessons your unique story teaches you.

Be efficient With so much work to do, make it a little easier. Batch up similar tasks so you can tackle them all at once. Create a process.

Take life a day at a time You may be so focused on your future goals, that you never take the time to pause and ask yourself what you really want, or to even open your eyes to the beauty around you. Be here now.

Do something new Make small changes to your routine, and little by little, life will regain colour. Try something new, however tiny, every day. Get lunch from a new place, take a different route to work, speak to a new person. Inject your life with some much-needed novelty.

QUEEN OF PENTACLES

UPRIGHT
comfort · luxury · status
prestige · dependable
generous · friendly · nurturing

REVERSE
jealous · frivolous
insecure · deprived
unkempt · self-centred

UPRIGHT

REVERSE

Interpretation

The Queen of Pentacles has a lavish home, meticulously kept with great taste. She appreciates the arts and the finer things in life. Her extravagance can be intimidating, but she is generous and welcoming. A warm, realistic, and practical woman, she never fusses about taking matters into her own hands. She is capable and self-made, working hard to make her dreams come true.

Reversed, this Queen may be messy and unkempt. Gone is her beautiful sanctuary. She can be jealous and spiteful, unhappy to see others achieve. She takes great pride in her material possessions, even if they are in disrepair, as she depends on them to combat her inner feelings of worthlessness. She neglects both self and others; they are mirror images of her despair.

Reflection

This Queen knows her needs and pursues them without apology. What are your emotional, physical, and spiritual needs? Do you have a healthy relationship with them? Sometimes, others can see pursuing our own needs as selfish. But how does having our own needs satisfied give us room to be more generous and giving to others?

Have you learnt to serve the needs of others without addressing your own? You may repress those needs and lash out in the form of tantrums and manipulation. What needs have you been hiding from your partner, your family, or your colleagues? How can you ask for them while respecting the boundaries and the agency of others?

Action

Be resourceful Make the best of what you have. Don't focus on what is lacking, think of what you need and how to get it with what you do have. Do you want to create something but don't have the tools? Make the tools! Want to make a recipe, but don't have the ingredients? Find a substitute!

Simplicity is key Spare yourself the trouble or the drama. Don't focus on the petty things, but on getting things done in a straightfoward manner. A common-sense approach can be helpful right now.

Take care of yourself It's not vanity – our bodies mirror our inner world. When we see someone who is well groomed, they exude confidence. When you take care of your body, you develop confidence.

Curate your environment Take some time to clean and organize your physical surroundings. An organized environment creates clear thoughts.

Create a care routine Work from the outside in. Clean your home once a week, clear out your wardrobe once a month, dress up every day.

KING OF PENTACLES

UPRIGHT
protector · provider
principled · traditional
conservative · ambitious

REVERSE
exploitative · possessive
materialistic · corrupt
unyielding

UPRIGHT

REVERSE

Interpretation

This King has always been determined and industrious, even as a child. Now he is a self-made man who has built an empire from his passions. He has learnt that wealth cannot buy true happiness – but it can buy freedom, safety, and comfort for himself, his family, employees, and community. He trusts, cares, and pays his workers well. In turn, they are loyal and admire his leadership.

In reverse, the King has fallen on hard times. He made risky business decisions that led him to ruin. He becomes stingy both in his material and emotional life; he dislikes spending money, effort, or feelings on himself or others. Relationships become transactional, and his family feels dull, cold, and distant. He has lost his vitality, now sickly in body and spirit.

Reflection

To grow in all aspects of our lives, we need to feel free to make mistakes, be vulnerable, and take risks. It is difficult to do this in an environment that is harsh and unforgiving. What gives you a feeling of safety? Do you have anyone – maybe a partner or family member – who makes you feel you'll always be safe?

What happens when you lose respect for your resources? When we don't understand something's true worth, we can be wasteful or abuse its power. Who or what have you been taking for granted? How has that affected how you treat them? What happens when we stop caring about a relationship, a skill or talent, or a cherished object?

Action

Create a feeling of security When we are afraid, it can be hard to make the right choices. Consider ways you can make yourself feel safe and protected right now.

Serve To have power is also to serve. If you find yourself in a place of influence, proceed from a place of love. Responsibility born from love creates a solid foundation.

Use resources wisely Know what you value and be a good steward of your life; that includes your material resources, emotional resources, and your energy.

Appreciate what you have Be grateful for all you have and see how it changes the way you treat your material things.

Check your possessiveness Protectiveness can easily turn to possessiveness if not managed. Being overly controlling towards someone can be an indication that you consider others as objects to be owned, not people.

Beware of ruthlessness You may be tempted to do things as quickly as possible, regardless of hurting others along the way. This won't be a sustainable path to success.

INDEX

ABOUT THE AUTHOR

Tina Gong is a tarot enthusiast, illustrator, and self-taught developer based in New York. She holds a BA from the Gallatin School of Individualized Study at NYU, where she studied linguistics. Her study of the structure of languages, alongside a lifelong interest in symbol, mythology, Jungian psychology, and esotericism, has led her towards the tarot, which she started using at a young age to help her learn more about herself, connect with others, and connect with the world around her. Prior to Labyrinthos, she also developed the controversial HappyPlayTime, a sex-education game and app, as well as working in design for companies with feminist missions. She has illustrated and designed a number of tarot decks, including the Golden Thread Tarot. Alongside her tarot decks, she has created accompanying apps, with the hope of adapting the tarot for modern lifestyles. Her hope is to help make tarot a resource for self-introspection, self-understanding, and acceptance that can be available for people from all walks of life to benefit from.

ACKNOWLEDGMENTS

This book wouldn't have been possible without the kind support of my husband, Luis, whose constant encouragement has remained steadfast throughout, even as I pestered him into coming with me to various classes and workshops on tarot and its related subjects, and who has also taught me so much about what it means to accept and love oneself and others.

Thanks are also given to my mother, who gave me her ferocity, persistence, determination, and fighting spirit. As well as my aunt Min, from whom I inherited my love for all things spiritual and metaphysical.

A big thank you also goes out to the publishing team at DK Books, with a special thanks to editor Emma Hill for her gentle and considerate support throughout the entire process. As a shy and soft-spoken person, this author is very grateful for having her as a liaison throughout. And finally, to managing editor Dawn Henderson, designer Tessa Bindloss, and the remainder of the design team for putting up with this author's finicky nitpicking, and for the detailed artistic feedback that pushed me to always do better. In the end, I could not have dreamed of more beautiful pages to come from this book.

SOURCES

Rachel Pollack *78 Degrees of Wisdom.* Weiser Books, 2019
Robert Place *The Tarot, Magic, Alchemy, Hermeticism, and Neoplatonism.* Hermes Publications, 2017
Eileen Connolly *Tarot: A New Handbook for the Apprentice.* Weiser Books, 2008
Frederick David Graves *The Windows of Tarot.* Morgan & Morgan, 1973
Papus *The Tarot of the Bohemians.* Wilshire Book Co, 1982
Wouter J. Hanegraff *New Age Religion and Western Culture: Esotericism in the Mirror of Secular Thought.* State University of New York Press, 1998
Ronald Decker, Thierry Depaulis, Michael Dummett "A Wicked Pack of Cards: The Origins of the Occult Tarot"
Sherryl E. Smith "Tarot History Chronology" [web article]
https://tarot-heritage.com/history-4/tarot-history-chronology/